SALES SECRETS

of a Five-Year-Old

Because Nobody Has a Better Close Ratio!

MIKEAL R. MORGAN

Original chapter introduction artwork by Paris Cudini - @pariscudini_art_

(Paris was 15 years-old at the time these drawings were created.)

Cover designed by Addam Cody Minuteman Press Houston West.

14838 Park Row Dr. Suite D - Houston, TX 77084 – 832-321-4380

Edited by Ann Kellett - https://www.annkellettcommunications.com

Mikeal R. Morgan

Visit my website at www.mikealmorgan.com to learn more about how to bring this program to life for your organization in a fun, highly interactive keynote or full training.

Printed in the United States of America

First Printing: 2020

© Published by Phoenix Training Innovations - 2020

ISBN-9781709000331

We were all born with the innate ability to be expert salespeople. But things happen that turn us into fearful, callous, overthinkers who sometime struggle to get results. It is time to take a step back, re-examine and truly embrace the traits and skills we were born with so we can realize our true potential as salespeople.

I would like to thank my personal, pint-sized instructors who helped teach me these lessons and so many others. I love you, Skyler, Brendin, Cameron, Trinity, and Mia!

STUFF WE WILL TALK ABOUT

INTRODUCING THE FIVE STEPS

We have all been in sales in some form our entire life, whether it's selling Mom or Dad on dessert before dinner, wearing what we want or the ultimate victory of staying up another thirty minutes past bedtime! No one has a better close ratio than a five-year-old kid! As we grow older, we continue selling our ideas and ourselves for relationships, job interviews, or for many of us, selling goods and services professionally.

But too often, something happens along that journey that impedes our results, in that we learn dreadful things like laziness, fear, ego and damaging pride. You may be thinking that these do serve some purpose and you would be right, but an imbalance keeps us from reaching our goals. Fear, for instance, keeps us from getting hurt in certain scenarios, but I would argue that it also stifles growth and goal obtainment a lot more than it saves us from danger. After all, you can be careful and safe, but is hard to be fearful and successful.

I have spent a lifetime in sales and leadership and have achieved some of the highest honors possible in both categories. I have also had the privilege of raising five children, and while the highest honor you can receive as a parent is stress, anxiety and losing your hair, I'd say that I have also achieved the highest honors in this category, as well!

I have used the methods I will teach you in this book to successfully exceed sales targets for more than twenty years and have done so without ever missing an annual sales target. I have also written five books; *How to Build Giants*, my first book on leadership, became a national best-seller in the United States.

As far as proof of my parenting success, I can only offer that my kids are happy, productive and love me, and that is pretty great by any standards!

So why did I write this book? Because learning to sell doesn't have to be so damned hard!

For decades, while I embraced the simple, fun, good-natured side of selling and how easy learning it can be, I watched companies create complex sales programs, one after the other, only to confuse and dishearten would-be sellers. These companies would write complex formulas, with many pages of acronyms and long, drawn-out processes that salespeople would *not* remember, much less use.

I am not saying that selling is easy, but learning to sell should be.

For decades, I have studied the parallel between how kids are so naturally good at selling, and the tactics of successful sales professionals. I have identified the "childish" traits and skills that consistently put successful sales professionals at the top of their game. Using both what makes kids and top sales professionals successful, I created a very simple, five-step process that teaches you everything from how to uncover new opportunities, to how to successfully close the sale and serve the client after the sale.

You may be thinking, *is following a structured sales process right for me?* My research suggests that following a sale process of any kind increases not only your results, but also the consistency and accuracy of forecasting those higher results.

The research also showed significant revenue increases at the company level for organizations that trained both their sales teams and sales managers on a defined sales process.
Two examples: a study published in *Harvard Business Review* showed that companies that mastered just three specific parts of a sales pipeline process experienced up to a 28% increase in revenue as compared to those that do not. Another study by a TAS Group and summarized in their Dealmaker Index Study found that 70% of organizations using a structured sales process are "high performers" and that over 70% of forecasts were more accurate for companies with a defined sales process.

Here are a few ways that a defined sales process can help you personally:

Make higher commissions. Salespeople aren't just in "it" for the thrills; we want to make money! A defined sales process will allow you to uncover and convert more opportunities than not using one because it helps you be more thorough and not have to rely solely on trying to remember to ask the right questions or say the right things.

Work smarter, not harder. People who use a road map or GPS get to their destinations faster and easier than those who do not. You will also get a very accurate ETA when using GPS that is difficult to accurately calculate otherwise. Following a sales process is similar to using a map or GPS in that it guides you and the prospect down a clear path where you both win in the end. If you follow it correctly, it allows you to forecast sales with extreme accuracy.

Have fewer stalled or lost deals. A good, defined sales process will first help you focus on finding good, qualified prospects that have a higher propensity of buying from you. These prospects are more likely to flow through the process without getting hung up along the way. Solid sales processes allow you to walk the prospect through a series of qualification and discovery points in order to expose all areas where you can help, and the pain associated with those opportunities, allowing the prospect to see value and to commit quickly and without remorse.

Sales processes that work long-term are ones that are *simple* to follow and *customizable* for your personality and your industry. I focused on these elements when designing the five-step process outlined in this book.

---

*"If you do not have a defined process that moves your people forward
so they can achieve greater results, then what is it you are managing?"*

– *Keith Rosen*

The Five-Step Process

Kids are naturally loud, honest, kind, true and fearless. Successful sales professionals understand that the basic skills and traits of being genuinely nice, honest and having integrity would make people trust them and want to buy from them. Both are fearless hunters, always finding a way to 1. **Uncover** opportunity, while loudly promoting themselves and their brand.

Kids make having fun a priority, are passionate about everything they do and enthusiastically welcome people. Successful sales professionals have fun and enthusiastically connect with prospects and 2. **Open** a call with passion and purpose.

Kids will wear you out asking questions because they are genuine and naturally curious. Successful sales professionals are genuinely curious and ask what seem like a million questions to uncover and 3. **Understand** what is important to people and how they could play a role in using their products and services to help.

Kids inherently know love and can connect easily and want best friends forever. They care about making people happy and winning. They express their feelings with passion and vigor and relentlessly negotiate for what they want. Success happens similarly for sales professionals when they align and 4. **Partner** with clients for long-term success through powerful and moving presentations and shrewd negotiations that benefit both parties. Strong relationships are established and rooted in personal connection, not just business transactions.

And finally, kids are never too bashful or prideful to selflessly serve others. In fact, they take pride in it. Sales professionals who are never too proud to humbly and attentively 5. **Serve** clients have long-term successful relationships that yield years of fruitful results and referrals to other clients, and tend to have successful and less stressful sales careers.

This proven, simple, five-step process is the same one that has been used by children and successful sales professionals for years.

In this book, I will teach you how to regain some of these traits that may be suppressed, and sharpen some of the skills that may be dull, so that you, too, can reach new levels of sales success. I will also do my very best to teach you a few new things in the most fun and entertaining way possible. While this book focuses primarily on business-to-business (B2B) sales, anyone in sales or considering a career in sales will benefit from the content! The content can even benefit buyers who want an advantage while buying.

I hope this book takes you back to a simpler time and place where you can think clearly about what will make you successful and let you smile a little while doing it! In the end, I hope that you come to the same realization that I did—if we stay true to the same simple, honest and fun approach to selling that we did as kids, we will experience a similar close ratio as we did back then. **Because nobody has a better close ratio than a kid!**

* * *

WARNING: Don't be fooled by the fun, light-hearted title or graphics. This book can cause excessive increases in professionalism, commission payouts, market expansion and personal growth!

Here is a visual of the Sales Secrets of a Five-Year-Old, Five-Steps©.

1. Uncover Opportunities
2. Open a Sales Call
3. Understand the Prospect
4. Partner for Success
5. Serve After the Sale

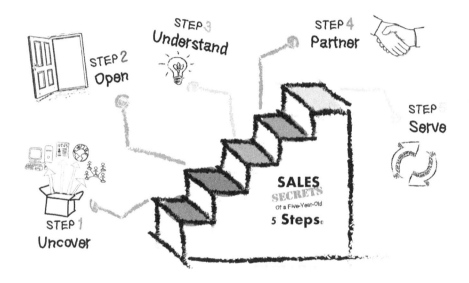

I will walk you through each of these steps, carefully outlining the basic traits and skills that kids use as a baseline. I'll then translate these into a more detailed, professional skill set you can deploy to successfully navigate each step.

This chart outlines both the basic skills and traits and the more detailed, professional skill sets.

Go Where other Kids are - Fearless - Relentless - Ambitious
Get Attention (Loud) - Embrace Technology

**PROSPECT FOR POTENTIAL CLIENTS -
MARKET YOURSELF - SET APPOINTMENTS –
USE SFA/CRM**

STEP 1
Uncover

Differentiate – Prideful - Excited - Visual - Structured

**OPEN A SALES CALL – BUILD RAPPORT –
SET THE STAGE TO SELL**

STEP 2
Open

Naturally Curious - Ask a Million Questions
Discover the what, when, why, how and who

**ASK STRATEGIC QUESTIONS - UNDERSTAND THE
PROSPECT'S BUSINESS PROBLEMS -
CREATE URGENCY – BUILD THE FUNNEL**

STEP 3
Understand

Optimistic - Story Tellers - Closers (Are we there yet?)
Proud Presenters - Shrewd Negotiators

**MATCH PROBLEMS TO SOLUTIONS – TELL THE
STORY - PRESENT - PROPOSE – NEGOTIATE – CLOSE**

STEP 4
Partner

Competitive – Creative – Perfectionist - Capacity to love

**FOLLOW UP - SERVICE AFTER THE SALE –
RELATIONSHIP BUILDING**

STEP 5
Serve

Finding Other Kids to Play With

STEP 1: UNCOVERING OPPORTUNITIES

"When I wanna play soccer, I look for other kids that maybe wanna play soccer too." – Mia (age 5)

In this step, you will learn how to uncover opportunity with the right type of prospects. You will also learn the importance of being ambitious and marketing yourself while using technology to track and improve your progress. You will also learn that you must ask for referrals and be fearless on the phone.

"Since you want to play soccer and I have a soccer ball, maybe we can play together?" – Kids are problem solvers!

Kids naturally want to be where other kids are and will actively seek other kids who are playing or have the propensity to play games they are interested in. If they want to play dolls, they go to the home of the girl who has the most or best dolls. If they want to play soccer, they go to the soccer field. In short, they go where there is like-minded enthusiasm.

Likewise, as a sales professional, you must be willing to actively seek out people (prospects) who want to play the same game you are playing— who are buying what you are selling. To do that, you should seek out people with *problems*! Finding fertile sales ground doesn't have to be as hard as most of us make it. Kids with no one to play ball with will seek out other kids who want to play ball but have no ball. This way, the problem is solved for both parties. You can do the same. Think at a high level about what problems your product or service solves, then seek companies and people with those problems.

It is easier to sell water to those who are thirsty!

"I get to go to school today!" – Kids are optimistic!

I remember getting my kids ready for school when they were young and they would say "Daddy, I am so excited that I get to go to school today!" One of the big things we lose the older we get is optimism. As kids, we say we *get* to do things, versus when we get older and responsibility, fear and pessimism mount, and we *have* to do things.

Prospecting is critical to your survival and success as a sales professional and few look forward to it. In fact, I don't personally know anyone who looks forward to it. But when I started thinking of prospecting as something that I got to do, versus something I had to do, it took on a different meaning. I was fortunate enough to sell alongside some folks who like me and who didn't have very much growing up and valued the opportunity to make money. These friends taught me that we could be the masters of our own destiny by figuring out the whole prospecting thing.

The best example of this for me was in the 1990s, when I sold mobile phones. I learned so much when I partnered with a guy named Eric, who always seemed eager to hit the streets to uncover opportunity. While Eric hadn't mastered the art of the pitch, or even the best way to introduce himself, his company or his intentions, he had mastered the ability to be completely optimistic about hitting the streets and knocking on prospective clients' doors. He literally expected each person to listen to him and accept an appointment with him.

On the first day I spent with him, I watched him smile so big as he walked through the door of business after business, boldly asking to speak to the person who paid the bills. He then went into why he worked for our company and explained that he was local to the neighborhood and had grown up in the local schools and how he was confident that he could help their business, and so on. He would end by optimistically asking for an appointment to discuss business. We had more success setting sales appointments that day than I had alone in any given month.

When I asked Eric what his secret was, he smiled and said, "No secret. We *get to* go out and talk to people every day if we want to. We are not stuck behind a desk and most of these people are so nice. Then we get to sell them stuff and make money!" What I learned from Eric that day was to stop being pessimistic about someone turning me down, telling me that there was no soliciting allowed or worse, uttering that dreaded word *no*. Instead, I had to start being completely optimistic about the entire approach. Eric was genuine and knew why he was doing what he was doing, but above all, he was hopelessly *optimistic.* It works for kids, it worked for Eric and it started working for me, as well!

Up early like it is Christmas morning! – Kids are not lazy!

When my kids were little, we would have to warn them not to wake up at four o'clock on Christmas morning to open gifts. They were highly motivated to wake up early and for the most part, most young kids are a lot of things, but lazy isn't one of them, especially in the morning.

Have you ever said, or heard someone say, "Oh, I'm not lazy. I am just not a morning person"? It's cool if you have, but from what I have observed, there is really no such thing as a *morning* person. There is such a thing as a *motivated* person, however, like a child on Christmas morning. It isn't that kids naturally wants to get up early, but on that morning, they are highly motivated. Kids have tons of energy and if channeled appropriately, the results can be great—and this is true for adults, too.

The most successful sales professionals I have seen—and I lump myself in this category—are up early and start work an hour or more before most others. They understand that to think, plan and execute as hard as needed on any given day will take extra time if they want to do it well. You aren't too tired or genetically disposed to wake up later—you are simply unmotivated. Maybe your job or the company you work for has made you uninspired. OR, before you quit your job, would you be more motivated and happier if you were determined to be better at what you do and became significantly more successful?

I don't mean to drop such *hard* truths on you so early in this book, but the truth is, sales is hard work. It's also extremely rewarding if done right and can provide so much motivation that you will be ready and willing to get up earlier to be successful.

One day, while working for the same telecommunications company where I met Eric, I met another guy who taught me how getting up early was helpful in sales, especially when you had certain deficiencies. Since the company expected us to be at the office by 8 a.m., I would arrive no later than about 7:45. I would get my prospecting list prepared and my day lined out.

One day, after a busy week of sales appointments, I needed to catch up on things, so I went into the office at about 6 a.m. When I got there, I saw a light burning in the corner cube and walked over to see who got to the office that early. That is where I met Brent.

I said, "Hey man, who are you and what are you doing here?"

"I'm Brent and I'm certainly not baking cakes!" he said, somewhat surprised. "I am working. Who are you and what are you doing?"

I laughed and apologized for crude introduction. We started talking and I asked if he got to the office every morning that early and why I hadn't seen him before.

He said, "I know who *you* are. You are very good. You lead the office in sales because you have the gift of gab. I don't—in fact, I am not very good at all. But sales is fair. I don't have to be as good as you are, I just have to work more hours than you do for the same or better results. I literally start my day early and am gone by the time you get here so I can get out there and start selling. And because of that, I am about to catch you in the rankings!"

And I'll be damned if he wasn't right. I was about to surrender my number-one spot to a guy who admitted he wasn't as good as I was. The bottom line is he didn't have to be—he only had to out-work me. Stay motivated, get up early and out-work those you can't out-sell!

"Can we go? Can we go? Can we go? Can we go?" – Kids are relentless!

When was the last time someone referred to you as absolutely relentless? Kids win most "sales" through sheer persistence. They know what they want, and they stick to it.

It's as if, as kids, we are hard-wired to stay on a mission and persist until we get a *yes*. Even though we understand that we risk annoying the person we seek something from, as a kid, we will remain so persistent that most people will concede due to being worn down or out of admiration of our persistence.

The goal of a sales professional is to persist and achieve the latter. People and businesses get spam solicitations through calls, emails and social media hundreds of times each week. We will talk more about how to stand out from the noise in a bit, but for now the lesson is persistence. Kids win sales by staying with it in the most relentless manner possible—and so should you.

Consistent, proper messaging and follow up, relentlessly executed, will help you win more sales—period.

If you start to get worn down from being so persistent, consider this: toddlers fall hundreds of times when learning to walk and never think, *maybe this walking thing just isn't for me!*

Kids don't want just some—they want it all! – Kids have big goals!

Kids will set, big audacious goals for anything and everything. They don't want just some—they want it all! If a kid wants to play football, they don't go find just one person; they go door to door recruiting a team. And in sales, you can't be successful if you don't first have prospects.

A prospect is simply a client that has not *yet* bought goods or services from you. An ideal prospect is someone with a high propensity to buy from you. So, how do you find ideal prospects? You start by setting the big goal of finding a lot of people with a high propensity to buy from you! You should find five, 10 or 20 times the number of people you actually intend to sell to.

If you are in *outside* sales, have you set goals for how many prospects you will target and convert, as well as where and how you will target them? Building and working through a list of prospects is critical. If you are in more of an *inside* sales role, you still need to market your local business in bold and new ways.

In today's world of social media, radio, and television, messages are quickly drowned out and lost. You must be calculating and think big when setting goals. Write your prospecting goals down now. How many prospecting attempts will you make each day and with what expectation? Where and how will you prospect? If via telephone, how many dials will it take you to actually speak to someone? How will you track your calls and emails and the conversions of those attempts to further the sale? How will you find more qualified prospects? Set and track your goals and make sure they are big enough!

2 + 2 = 4 – Kids practice math!

One of the most important things you learn when you are a kid is how to properly solve math problems. As sales professionals, we tend to have sharp math skills when calculating commissions checks, but sometimes forget how important math is when prospecting.

Do you know your numbers? If you call yourself a full-time sales professional, you should practice your math, too, because if you can't measure it, you can't improve it. What is your call to appointment ratio? How different is it from your email to appointment ratio? How many appointments can you convert to a quote or proposal? How many quotes/proposals do you produce before you convert to a sale? Do you know how many units/products an average sale will yield? If you track these ratios, you can do some great things. You can focus on what you are good at and do more of it, and you can also work on what you suck at and work on improving those gaps. Now the question is, how do you effectively track these statistics?

"If you can't measure it, you can't manage it." – Peter Drucker

---

Here is an example of a tracker I have successfully used. By inputting five variables that every sales professional should know and track on the left-hand side of the tracker, the right-hand side of sheet calculates how many calls, sales appointments, proposals and deals I should produce each month to reach my goals. On the bottom right, it also calculates my ratios for my call, appointment and close ratios. This calculator and other resources can be downloaded at www.mikealmorgan.com

Sales Secrets Ratio Improvement Tracker®

Enter 5 variables based on your current state in the yellow cells below			Required Monthly Activity to Achieve Goals (Based on current State)	
How many Calls	Equals	Appointments	Calls Required	635
12		1	Appointments Required	53
How many Appointments	Equals	Proposals	Proposals Required	18
3		1	Closed Won Deals Required	6
How many Proposals	Equals	Deals		
3		1	**Ratios**	
Average Deal Size in Units			Calls to Appointments Ratio	8%
17			Appointment to Proposal Ratio	33%
Monthly Unit Goal			Close Rate	33%
100				

SALES SECRETS Of a Five-Year-Old ©

As I improve my call to appointment ratio, fewer calls are required to reach my goals. The same goes for appointment to proposal and proposal to closed sale ratios. This tracker proves what I believe about sales being fair, because it shows that if I am not proficient in one area, I can improve proficiency in another and still reach the same goal.

Let's play a video game! – Kids embrace technology!

I loved playing video games when I was a kid. I would pop a game in the first time and start mashing every button on the controller until I noticed what each function did. Those first several games, I would lose big time! I would get killed in seconds and have to start all over again.

But as I failed again and again, I found new ways to get better and better. Small adjustments gave me a slight edge until one day, I would begin to master the game, win more and navigate the screens and characters with ease. The more I used the systems and games, the better I became, so much so that I could make quick work of most of my competition. As we get older and access different systems, especially ones we are not comfortable with, we too often are scared to push buttons and try different things, as if we are going to mess something up or lose.

But kids are not intimidated by technology, and you shouldn't be, either! As a kid, you were not intimidated to play and even lose a video game while learning to be very good at it. Using technology to prospect is imperative in today's competitive climate. Even if you use it and lose for a while, so what?

Read and research ways to leverage things like social media, customer relationship managers (CRM) and sales force automation (SFA) in order to not only leverage it but to force multiply your efforts. Simply put, technology allows us to do more with less. How much time have you devoted to pushing buttons, reading books or doing on-line learning about the systems that could help take you to the next level of sales? Have you created a strategy around how you will use the system to improve your results?

Take the time to become an expert on whatever system you use (or are supposed to use) so that you can become more efficient and effective. And if you lose, the good news is that you can start over!

17

"I'll do it!" – Kids are born fearless!

Fear isn't something we are born with. This is evident when you hold a baby, and if the baby gets tired or restless, they will typically begin to fling themselves back and forth, without fear of falling or being dropped. The child is ignorant of the danger of falling; he or she just moves in the way that seems right. We learn fear and most of what we fear is simply the anticipation of being hurt, and most of this is from what we have heard may hurt us, not from first-hand experience.

The weird thing that most sales professionals don't face danger or even fear pain, but fear things like simple rejection. Kids win sales because they are unafraid to go after what they want. They aren't at all bothered by being told *no*, because they know they will simply persist until *no* turns into a *yes*.

Rejection is something we fear because it makes us uncomfortable, not because it is actually dangerous. It sounds silly when you think about the fact that for most sales professionals, the fear of being told *no* outweighs the possibility of being told *yes* and getting the sale. You must come to grips with rejection and accept it as a part of the profession. I have been told *no* thousands of times—and that was when I was dating! In sales, I've been rejected hundreds of thousands of times, yet still managed to succeed at both dating and sales!

"Let's start a lemonade stand!" – Kids are natural entrepreneurs!

My little girl started a lemonade stand in our neighborhood one day when she was nine years old. We made a gallon of lemonade and had a package of chocolate chip cookies on a table and she made $33 in about three hours. Why—because of her gourmet offerings?

No, it was because she held a sign up high for everyone to see. She let people close to her know that she was selling something and that they could help. People close to us will help if they know our cause. Are you active on social media platforms like LinkedIn and Facebook?

18

Does your circle of friends and family know what you sell? Have you sent a text to everyone in your contact list asking for referrals or business? Most people close to us want to help us, but unless you "hold the sign up high" they may not know to help.

"Mom, Mom, Mom, Mom, Mom!" – Kids are born loud and get heard above the noise!

Okay, I will admit that while this one is a tad annoying, it is extremely effective. Kids naturally know that the more noise they make, the more attention they will get, good or bad. As we get older, we understand that we can't just go screaming anytime we want something, and we become more and more quiet. If we remain quiet long enough, we start to lose that ability to get loud and be heard. When is the last time you went campaigning for business? When is the last time you got a little *loud*? I am not advocating screaming and yelling at folks, but think of the right way, place and people to get *loud* in front and get your brand noticed.

Loud could be wearing clothes that have your logo or brand and doing volunteer work. *Loud* could be posting images and video on social media while you are out prospecting. *Loud* could also mean speaking up a little more about what you do and why.

I tried and failed to be loud for months when I first started in sales. I attended various community networking lunches where you were encouraged to stand up and give a short introduction of yourself and how you helped people. As much as I wanted to gain from them, I always walked out disappointed by the lack of qualified leads I generated. I knew my pitch was weak and that I wasn't reaching people.

That changed when a mentor of mine challenged me to be loud in the right way if I wanted bigger results. He said if I wanted to get more from these meetings, then I should be prepared to put into them as much as I expected to get out of them.

He challenged me to spend time crafting a great value proposition (something you will learn about shortly) and to practice saying it until it sounded smooth and natural. He then tasked me not just to speak about the value that I could add, but to add specific value that would benefit the attendees.

I went through and called every contact I had to find qualified leads in almost every industry I could find. At the next networking meeting, I was prepared not only to be loud, but to add real value. I stood and proudly gave my value proposition and announced that I had about 24 leads that I would be handing out after the meeting to help others grow their business, and would appreciate it if they would be willing to help me, as well. I remember calling down over 60 leads that I got from that one event. Being loud for me was about adding value to others if I expected value in return.

"The right to be heard does not automatically include the right to be taken seriously." - Hubert H. Humphrey

---

"Wait until you hear what happened!" - Kids are great storytellers.

I want you to close your eyes and imagine the last really intense story you've heard a kid tell. Children tell such descriptive stories, and with excitement and passion. They can bring you to the place they are and make you feel the way they felt in that moment. It is so important to be a great storyteller when you are prospecting. Are you product pushing and annoying prospects with weak scripts when you call on them, or are you bringing them to another place and time where their business could use the product you sell to look, or be better, more profitable or productive?

Can you tell a story that uses colorful characters and mental images that put the prospect buying your product?

I will walk you through how to use storytelling later in the sales process, but the key to storytelling while prospecting is to keep the story at a high level and concise—no more than about a minute. You don't want the prospect looking at you like we look at kids who ramble and ramble until their funny story turns into "the story that never ends!" How are your storytelling skills? Have you worked on a short, high-impact story that you can tell while prospecting? Can you tell it with passion and conviction?

I have learned in sales that it is hard to be convincing without conviction.

"I see you like dolls, and so does my friend, Ashley. Let's go talk to her." – Kids are natural networkers!

Kids are natural networkers and build vast networks of friends. People buy from people they like and trust; when you are referred, it is one of the easiest and best ways to get connected to a prospect. I have watched my kids grow their networks through the years based primarily on their interests at the time. For instance, if one was interested in a certain sport, they found and were introduced to other friends with similar sports interests. They were also great at using those friends as resources to find new places to play, or friends to play with.

When it comes to uncovering sales opportunities, asking for referrals is a fantastic way to prospect. The leads are significantly warmer and about 60% more likely to close than cold leads. One of the most effective ways I have found to ask for referrals is to build a list! You literally type out a list of the businesses, people or even geographic areas or industries you most want to sell to. Next to the list, you mark a spot for name, phone number and email address. Build a near-complete list, carefully leaving about three blank spots at the bottom. (I'll explain in a minute.) Now that you have your list built, print it and carry it everywhere.

Start by asking your friends, family and best clients who they know on your list that they can connect you with.

If they say they don't know anyone on your list, say that it isn't a big deal, then point to your blank spots at the bottom and ask for names of people they do know! This way, in theory, you will be getting at least one referral or sales lead from everyone you know, because everyone knows someone. It's all about asking in a creative manner!

"Five more minutes, Mom?" – Kids use all of the time they have!

Kids play until the last minute, making the most of playtime because there are timelines given and, in some cases, visual indicators of that timeline to keep them honest. For me as a kid, the sun going down and the streetlights coming on let me know to head home.

The idea here is, are you using every minute you have allocated to do a certain task—specifically, prospecting? Have you dedicated time daily to prospect? I have noticed that a common downfall of many sales professionals is a lack of dedicated time spent prospecting. Some schedule time, only to use an incoming call, someone walking up to ask a question—any interruption at all—to not have to do the arduous task of cold calling prospects. It's much better to stay the course and focus on the task at hand.

Creating lists and prospecting is one of the most critical things you can do as a sales professional to change the game. I have seen many people in leadership roles (and even peers) step up to help a sales professional close a deal, but rarely have I seen someone prospect for a salesperson.

You have to want it more than you fear it. Set time on your calendar and treat it as a sales appointment you can't possibly miss. The other thing to do here is to schedule it daily and don't miss a day if you can help it.

I have seen salespeople fail when they schedule a prospecting activity just once or twice a week, only to have "something big come up" and blow them off. If you miss a day of prospecting, you are only a day behind and can catch up quickly. Catching up after missing a week is significantly harder.

"Kids have to do homework!"– Learning doesn't stop in the classroom for a child and shouldn't stop at the office for you. Do your homework!

Homework is something that most kids, especially young ones, actually look forward to. But as is the case with many of our childhood priorities, we often lose interest and find *better* things to do with our time the older we get, even if we still see value in it. And it's not that kids and some adults don't see value in homework. They know that homework enhances proficiency and knowledge or supplements learning gaps. The problem most folks—young or old—have is that homework must take place outside of "normal hours."

Regardless, as sales professionals, we need to take a page from kids on the homework practice if we are to improve our results. While kids may be asked to solve math problems or write a paper for homework, sales professionals should stick to more research-based projects. You should be regularly researching many things, not limited to the products you or your competitors sell. Study topics that will improve your odds of uncovering business opportunities.

Let's start with the big picture and think globally. Are you watching headline news, or subscribing to major news outlets that will let you know what is taking place around the world that may impact your prospect's business? These are big things like financial markets, wars, disease outbreaks or resource shortages. If you research and study these things, ask yourself how they could possibly impact your prospects or better help you leverage your product when calling on prospects. Will the spread of a war, for instance, put pressure on business production in a negative or positive way? For this research, use global news and finance websites, and news channels on television and other outlets.

Then let's explore vertically into the prospect's line of business. What things are going on in the prospect's vertical market that could impact, positively or negatively, the way the prospect or industry does business? Could a new law or mandate cause disruption or punitive risk if the client doesn't adjust the way they do business—and could you help? For this research, use industry trade magazines, web pages and organizations that cater to the vertical you are interested in, like industry associations, and so on.

Next, let's think geographically about where the prospect is physically located and where they conduct business. What things like weather events or local legislative outcomes could impact your prospect that you could call and ask them about? For this research, use local news sources and websites about the surrounding areas.

Research horizontally into the position of the prospect office you are calling. Can you find a common concern or need that affects everyone in that same position? For instance, if I am calling on sales directors, I know that they are all concerned with sales, but I may learn that the industry I am calling on is especially concerned about units sold versus revenue captured, thus allowing me to speak their language about this specific issue. For this level of research, you can use industry-specific websites as well as general business sites.

Finally, have you done homework on the specific company you are calling on? This must be managed tightly as you could spend more time researching than you do calling on prospects if you aren't efficient in your research efforts. But researching a specific company allows you to understand what is important to the company and the clients they serve. You can better understand its structure, leadership and even its mission/vision in many cases. In addition to visiting their website, also search for the company name to find any news articles about them. Look for things like people assuming new leadership roles, recent mergers, or trouble they may be in.

All these are useful when crafting your perfect pitch that will have the prospect listening to everything you say. I will continue to show you how to position this knowledge in the next few topics.

"My hair is brushed, and my bag is packed!" - Kids are prepared.

I can't speak for all kids, but when I was little, I discovered I have what I consider to be CDO. That's like OCD but I am so OCD that I have to alphabetize the acronym!

That's a joke, but I do consider myself extremely well organized and prepared. My kids and many others that I have observed are, as well. They know after doing something once or twice, what they will need and prepare accordingly going forward. Those who have a vested interest in or enjoy what they are doing or where they are going, fare better at preparation than those who are not pleased with the activity.

Children who enjoy school typically do not have to be dragged out of bed and will brush their hair and teeth and prepare their lunch without being reminded. Kids who love the sport they play will double check the car to ensure they have brought all of the gear they need, because they understand that if they forget something, the coach will more than likely not let them play.

It is often the same with adults, especially sales professionals. If we are going on a closing appointment, we tend to be very excited, double check the outfit we plan to wear, ensure the laptop is charged, and so on.

The question, however, is this: are you that prepared when you do something you dread, like prospecting? You must put the same effort into preparing for successful prospecting or you will have fewer and fewer meetings to close something at. As remedial as it may sound, you'll need to create a checklist of all of the things you need or should prepare for prior to leaving your home or office.

Double check that list and make a real effort to be as prepared as you can be. It's a self-fulfilling prophecy: you hate prospecting because you are unprepared, and you are unprepared because you hate prospecting. It is time to break the cycle.

"Can I call Grandma?"– Kids are fearless on the telephone; you should be, too.

Most little kids will grab a phone quickly and start talking. Especially young ones. They want to listen and usually also have a lot to say. Once we grow up, phones are used more for texting, social media, apps and avoiding robo-callers than they are for talking.

And yes, I have read the reports, studies and books that claim tele-prospecting is dead and how you shouldn't use this antiquated method. That is precisely why I am strongly encouraging you not just to use the phone, but to be a complete telephone badass! In my opinion, the reason so many people are against tele-prospecting is because they are unprepared, which increases their rejection rates. They are unable to pivot toward what will work better because they haven't tracked what is and isn't working.

Spend time studying and tracking the success and failures you have on calls. Tweak your words and ask provocative questions that get attention the second someone picks up. It took me failing a lot to get comfortable prospecting on the phone.

I had to realize that I needed to have a *conversation*, not a sales call.

But first, I had to break the conditioned response of the person who answered. A conditioned response is an automatic response to an ordinarily neutral stimulus established through training. In lay terms, it means the shit people automatically say when they should probably wait until they fully understand the situation—but don't.

This conditioned response is most noticeable when you pass someone in a hallway and say, "How are you?" They will almost instinctively respond with, "Fine, and you?" It is an involuntary process that must tactfully but effectively be broken if you are to have success over the phone.

I conducted a social experiment years ago in which I walked down the unfamiliar halls of the office building where I worked. I didn't know anyone and would greet the first several people with the typical "Hey, how are you?" pleasantries. As expected, they responded with a half-smile, a nod and a "Fine, thank you."

But for the next several individuals, I took a different approach. I smiled, nodded and said, "Hey, don't go outside!" Most all of them, after exhibiting the traditional and expected conditioned response of "Fine, thank you," would stop, look puzzled and say, "Wait a second—what do you mean by that? Is there something bad out there that will hurt me? Or, is there something outside that is good, you just don't want me to get?"

I would smile and let them know I was just trying to see if they were paying attention or if they just figured I was politely saying hello. They all agreed that they anticipated what I was going to say and responded almost involuntarily. Only after processing what I actually said did they respond appropriately.

This happens every time we start a prospecting call with "Hello, how are you today?" The prospect's brain goes into conditioned response mode and says something like, "We are happy—and no thanks" as they hang up. We do it each time someone calls us with an uninvited solicitation, mispronouncing our name or asking about our day, right? And with the rise of robocalls, we can't blame them but blame our own conditioned responses and weak approach!

Break the conditioned response by not first asking about them or their day. Sure, you are nice, but you are not a psychologist and can't fix what you are asking about, so why ask? Let me give you an example.

If I call and say "Hello, how are you today?" and they answer with "Terrible! My dog bit me and my coffee is cold. What are you going to do about it?" You can only apologize and hang up (traumatized, and without a sale or sales appointment, might I add).

You, however, are a business professional and could ask about business. For instance, if you ask, "How is business?" and they respond with "Great! It's never been better!" then you could say, "Excellent—I couldn't have called at a better time." Conversely, if they say "It's terrible—never been worse!" then you could respond by saying, "Then I couldn't have called at a better time." However they respond, you are okay because you kept it about business and steered them away from the conditioned response by asking a question they weren't expecting.

Other questions are also powerful. Pick the top one or two things your product or service will help the prospect with, based on your homework, and ask about what they are currently doing around those things. This may even be what is referred to as an anxiety question, in that when it is asked, it gives the person asked a bit of anxiety. For instance, if I were calling (and I do) to sell the book you are reading or the live training program that I facilitate based on this book, I would ask, "Will your current conversion rate of sales calls to proposal ratio enable you to exceed your annual sales targets?"

Obviously, the person answering the phone won't typically know the answer, so they will feel inclined to transfer me to the person I am requesting to speak with, who is responsible for those things. In my case, I am looking for sales or C-level leaders who care about sales. Prepare your questions in order to break the conditioned response, so you will get attention and be transferred to those responsible for what it is you sell. Through preparation and practice, you will begin experiencing more success when tele-prospecting. These methods work well when walking into a business, in person, as well. And sometimes just having manners will get you the appointment.

"Please and Thank You!" – Kids have manners, and you should, too. It is the best way to WORK WITH the gatekeeper.

Manners are something I instilled in my kids from a very early age. I feel as if it sets a pace and tone for respect while keeping them humble. Every time my kids really wanted anything above and beyond the normal, they paid close attention to their manners. They made sure they said *please* and *thank you*, *yes sir* and *no sir*. In my overall experience and observations, kids who have manners "close the sale" much more often than those without.

But how do you apply this in a professional sales or prospecting environment? When you call a business to sell them on an appointment, you typically reach the person who answers the phone and, in most cases, does their darndest to keep from you from speaking with anyone at their company. These folks are often referred to as gatekeepers. If you paid close attention to the last few topics on breaking the conditioned response and having a lot to say, you will understand that gatekeepers are very prone to listening for the typical "Hello there, how are you?" so they can promptly and almost automatically launch their verbal assault regarding why you shouldn't call because they have plenty of whatever it is you are selling.

Some telemarketing books teach how to go around the gatekeeper or trick them in some way. I have had very little luck with this method but great success when I decided to work with them and simply have good manners. So, how do you leverage manners here after the conditioned response without continuing to get shut down?

Well, after you ask a very thought-provoking question that breaks the gatekeeper's conditioned response, you acknowledge that you are calling to set up a sales appointment, <u>BUT</u> (very important *but*) you really need *their help* in going about it <u>the right way, with the utmost respect for their process.</u>

I then usually ask if the person I am trying to reach keeps their own schedule or if the person I'm talking with keeps it for them. I let them know that I find it offensive when people call and try to play games, when I respect the process and would like to know the *best way to set the appointment*. I may even leverage the fact that most gatekeepers answer the phone with "COMPANY NAME, how may I help you?" I let them know that I am so glad they said how can they help me because I need some help setting an appointment the right way! This has been the most successful way for me of landing appointments both via the telephone or in person.

And it will work for you if you ask with conviction—you know, the way a child does. But what happens when you get the people you are calling for on the phone? You should have something prepared that they will want to hear! If you only knew what they wanted to hear about . . .

"How about a nice shoulder massage?"– Kids know what you want!

"Mom, you looked stressed, so how about a nice shoulder massage?" That was my go-to line anytime I needed something as a kid. My mom was a sucker for a great shoulder massage, and I knew it. I also knew that because she got them so infrequently, I could leverage them for something I needed. That is how kids are wired. They learn about what someone wants or needs and leverage their ability to deliver that in order to get what they want.

Keep in mind that while this may seem selfish, you can't help people if you don't know what they want. Salespeople aren't any different. Or at least, they shouldn't be.

The good news is that we covered much of the information you will need to gather if you want prospects to be interested in what you say, in the section about doing your homework!

But what happens if you don't have enough information? Isn't there stuff that all businesses are interested in? Yes! In fact, all prospects are primarily interested in three things. You will be using these three things throughout the sales process, so pay close attention.

I call them **FIP: Finance, Image and Productivity.**

All prospects care about FIP in some form or fashion. If you can position your product in a way that impacts the prospect's FIP, your chances of selling to them increase exponentially. All for-profit businesses are in business to make money (finance) and this can be impacted in many ways, like improving market share, increasing revenue or driving down costs. They also care greatly about how the public and their clients perceive them, (image) and are therefore always concerned about how fruitful their work is (productivity) as it tends to help the F and the I.

As important as it is to learn what is specifically important to them, learn how your product impacts your prospect's FIP so that you can add value to them by properly positioning your product to FIP.

Using what is known as a value proposition, I can position what I know about FIP, and how my product can help the prospect with one or all aspects of FIP to communicate a compelling reason for them to meet with me when prospecting, as well as when I open a sales call. You see, even if they do agree to meet with you, you must earn your spot in that meeting again once you get there, as well. You might use a value proposition in multiple places throughout the sales process.

Most of the old school sales books tell you to have (and practice) a value proposition or pitch of some sort. I used to think this was a bunch of bullshit because it sounded so canned. In fact, I could spot a canned value proposition a mile away. It turned out that what I was actually spotting was *unproperly* canned value proposition!

I figured that out when attending a sales conference and hearing the late, great Zig Ziglar say, "Everyone should have a canned sales pitch. If you can tell it's canned, it's just been improperly canned."

I looked at what I was doing and realized that I, too, had been using a canned value proposition for years, but was so comfortable saying it that it didn't feel, or sound, canned at all. While I believe in asking thought-provoking questions to break the conditioned response and to work with gatekeepers, at some point after asking a few questions and getting an attentive audience, you have approximately 20 to 30 seconds to state the reason you called—and it better be compelling!

If done well, it could even prompt them to invite other, more senior, members of their organization onto the call or into the meeting. This may allow you to progress the sale faster or on a larger scale. Through a well-crafted value proposition, you will begin differentiating yourself from just another salesperson to a value-added partner.

Here is how to create your value proposition:
1. Value propositions should take into consideration specific information that is important to the prospect, like the goals or initiatives you learn about in your homework. You can often learn these things on the company's website and through news articles or other online resources. Learn two to three things related to FIP that are important to the prospect from various sources, such as, *"We aim to deliver the best experience possible to our customers"*—or other catch phrases, goals or initiatives. These could even be business problems such as fines or failures where your product could make a difference.
2. Determine how your product can help the prospect solve the problems or meet those needs, goals or initiatives you've uncovered. Create examples of how you have helped other prospects, especially ones in the same industry or proximity. Adding statistics, facts, case studies or client recommendations that back up your claims is particularly helpful.
3. Craft a clear, compelling and concise value proposition that flows naturally.

4. Practice it until it feels and sounds natural, like something you would normally say. Don't use words you don't usually use, or you will be improperly canning your value proposition, and everyone will be able to tell, making it less effective!

5. Keep it focused on FIP but change it for each prospect based on the specific goals, wants, problems and needs you've learned about them.

6. End it with a question that gets you right into a dialog with the prospect. Don't ask if this is okay or if now is good time. Ask something pertaining to what you've learned about their company.

7. Always be honest in your claims.

When selling sales training to carpet cleaning companies, after breaking the conditioned response and getting a decision maker on the phone, I might say, "I called you on purpose today because I noticed your goals to expand operations into three new cities on your website. First of all, congratulations! And second, it seems like I called at a great time. I facilitate sales training programs that have helped carpet cleaning companies grow their business, improve market share, and increase sales by up to 23%. These companies also saw residual impacts like a 13% spike in referral business, all in just three short months after completing one of my programs. I wanted to discuss how we could help you get those same types of results and help you with your expansion goals. What city are you looking to expand in first?"

Again, I am using what I learned from their website, coupled with how my product can directly help. In this case, I focused primarily on the finance part of FIP from what I learned. Use these value propositions to establish value and to validate why the prospect should invest this time with you during this meeting.

Let me break down how and why my value proposition works. First, *"I called you on purpose."* This subconsciously takes down their defenses about being called off some list. I called them on purpose, not cold. They instantly—subconsciously—become more open to what I say.

Next, *"I noticed YOUR goals on your website."* Since that statement is so specific, it gets attention and has the listener focusing on what I am about to say.

I then tell them what it is I do (sales training) but more importantly, how this has helped a company in their same industry do things that they want to do, specifically *"grow their business, improve market share, and increase sales by up to 23%."*

I even give the exact percentage increases and timelines I was able to accomplish with the other company like theirs.

Finally, I asked a relevant question to keep them engaged.

You can have anything you want in life if you are willing to help other people get what they want." – Zig Ziglar

---

"Will there be cake?" – Kids ask a lot of direct questions!

"I see you are getting dressed. Are we going somewhere?" "Since we are going somewhere, what toys are they going to have there to play with?" "I am getting hungry, will there be cake?" These are the questions I would often get asked by my kids.

The art of asking question is perhaps the greatest sales skill a kid has. Kids are also smart, using information they obtain through various sources, and coupling that information with a question in order to learn more or uncover opportunity. One instance of this is when kids would come by the house to sell cookies at about 7:30 in the evening, saying,

"By the great smells coming from your house, you probably just ate dinner and need something sweet to finish off your meal, so how about some delicious cookies?" They used the information of scent and time of night to make assumptions and then asked a question to gain interest.

Kids use this method to be funny, like the time I dropped my drink in the kitchen and thought no one heard or saw my embarrassing accident, only to have my son ask about ten minutes later if I wanted him to get me something to drink. He said he would be sure to put it in a secured glass that had a lid. He said it to be funny, but still used the concept of using information coupled with a question, and this can be extremely effective while uncovering opportunities.

The most effective way to use this in a sales scenario is to use information you gathered during your homework that you know is a concern for the prospect and leverage it to your advantage with a question. If your research uncovered that a company is not meeting their expansion targets, and is using one of your competitors' inferior systems when your product or service could help them be better or faster, you might ask the decision maker, "How are you leveraging your current system to ensure you meet your expansion targets?" Knowing the answer is that they can't or it's not working to their expectation, or whatever the case may be, opens the door for you to pitch.

You can also ask questions about known, specific concerns about the competition's product or service levels that the prospect currently has in place. Pick ones for which you perform significantly better. For instance, if it is known that the prospect uses a competitor that has service calls that take a minimum of three days to schedule and therefore puts the prospect behind schedule, and if you can complete them in one day, you might call and ask the decision maker, "When all service calls are scheduled within the day with (competitor's name), does that help you stay on schedule and best serve your clients?"

Again, based on what we know, we can anticipate that the client will say something to the effect of, "I wish they could be scheduled in a day; it takes them three or more days. Why? Can yours be scheduled in a day? That would be a huge help."

There is your open door to pitch the benefit of scheduling service calls within one day instead of three, and any other relevant and applicable benefits of doing business with you.

We will discuss asking questions and curiosity in several places, but when it comes to using questions to uncover opportunity, kids thrive in this space—and so can you.

"But why not?" – Kids don't overthink!

What do rich people need, poor people have and if you eat it, you will die?

My mentor asked me that riddle when he caught me overthinking things. I asked him for the answer, and he told me that I should ask a child. He said that if I asked people with college degrees, they would fail to get the answer about 90% of the time, whereas a pre-teen child could answer it correctly almost 90% of the time.

I asked my daughter, who was nine years old, and after thinking about it for about a minute, she said, "Nothing! The answer is nothing, Dad. Rich people need nothing, poor people have nothing and if you eat nothing, you will for sure die!"

I had been schooled by a nine-year-old. I have written about the fact that that most adults overthink every chance they get, and even with all of the awareness I have about overthinking, I still find myself doing it, too. Kids just don't overthink like adults do. If they want something, they ask, and do it with an expectant attitude! When you are prospecting, you must not overthink, but instead go out and ask for it, with an expectant attitude.

"This stamp tastes yucky." – Kids write letters!

Kids are excited any time they get mail and typically love writing back, simply fascinated by the entire process of mail delivery. When I was a kid, receiving a birthday card from my grandmother was one of the highlights of my year. And sure, the five-dollar bill that was folded neatly inside helped, but more than anything, I loved that I got a piece of mail.

I would always write her back instead of just calling her to thank her, because I thought that she might be as excited as I was to get a letter in the mail.

Maybe it's the nostalgia of getting a card from grandma when we were kids or maybe it's because in today's world of technology and fast-paced hustle and bustle, most of the mail we receive is just bills and junk mail, that we still get excited to get mail as adults if it is hand addressed with our name on it. Statistics show that a direct-mailed, hand-addressed, handwritten card will be opened at the mailbox about 90% of the time, versus being brought inside to be sorted through with the other mail.

Furthermore, even when it is not opened at the mailbox, it will be opened before any of the other mail. So much technology is used today to connect to others, from social media, email and text messages, that mailing a letter has become a lost art of sorts. If you are serious about differentiating yourself from others and making a statement that is bold, memorable and gets attention, consider buying some stationery and stamps and taking ten minutes to write a nice note to a prospect that has not let you speak to the decision maker you requested. Think about it from a gatekeeper's perspective. The chances of them ever getting a piece of mail at work is minimal, at best. When they get a card that is addressed to them directly, and they open it and read:

> *"I never mean to be a bother when I call you asking to speak to Mr. Prospect. I just wanted to thank you for always being kind and polite to me when I call. The Prospect Company is lucky to have such a great employee representing them."*

When I, (the only sales professional to ever write them the only handwritten snail mail they have ever received at work) set my reminder and follow up with them the next week, what do you feel my chances of being transferred are? I'll put it this way: I have never regretted spending the money it costs me to mail a letter, ever.

And don't overthink this. It doesn't have to be some kind of long, elaborate letter. It can literally just be a few words like: *"Thank you for being so polite to me when I call."* Or, *"I wish every person that answered the phones I call were as kind as you are. Thank you!"*

The point is that you are reaching out in a way that touches someone's heart and differentiates you from others. Do what others only talk about. Make the time and prioritize writing a few cards each week and you will see how impactful it can be.

"Can I call you tomorrow?" – Kids follow up!

Kids are great about wanting to continue the conversation with anyone they start talking to, especially if there is unfinished business. When I was nine years old, I had a fascination with rocks and wanted a rock polisher more than anything. One Sunday, a very sweet lady at my church told me that she had one and would give it to me, and even promised to bring it the next Sunday.

The Monday after I was promised the rock polisher, I asked my mom if I could call this nice lady to remind her of her promise. My mom asked me to wait a day or so and said that we shouldn't bother her. Nevertheless, every night that week, I'd ask my mom if I could call this nice lady to see if we could get the rock polisher from her. My mom continued to deny my request until at last, Sunday arrived and as you can probably guess, I was up and ready to go to church nice and early.
The second I saw that nice lady, I ran up to her smiling from ear to ear, only to have her look down at me and say how sorry she was from not bringing my rock polisher, and that she really wishes I would have called her to remind her.

While Mom's heart was in the right place, perhaps allowing me to make one quick reminder call that Saturday evening would have saved me some heartache and not been a bother at all.

There is a way to follow up with prospects and clients that is both effective and non-intrusive. The best way, ideally, is to follow up the way the client prefers. You identify that preference by simply asking what, when and how you should follow up.

The process is a little different with a prospect in that most prospects are resistant to you calling them in the first place and would probably prefer you never follow up with them as they do not yet know the real value you offer. That said, it is important to keep a prospect follow-up file so that you can regularly follow up with all of the prospects you have uncovered. Keep in mind that calling them every day is usually only going to upset them, but call at least once per month to see if the person you called for originally is available or if anything has changed in their business that would prompt them to want to speak to you.

While it's best to send handwritten cards to prospects you can't reach, following up via phone or email with people you have already made first contact with is much more efficient and effective. Follow-up touches are just as critical as first touches. There is plenty of research that suggests that it can take as many five to eight touches before a prospect will agree to meet with a sales professional.

"Best day – ever!!!" Kids have fun!

Some of the most fun a kid can have is a taking a trip to the furniture store, tire shop, bank, or even the barber. These places are not meant to entertain kids, yet kids seem to have a ton of fun. The difference is the mindset a kid has—the determination to have fun. Making games out of the mundane and using what they have on hand to entertain themselves is a kid's specialty. It can be yours, too. Be determined to have fun and watch how your prospects respond. People buy from people. If you are miserable, your prospect can almost smell it.

Change your mindset and habits and you will change your results!

Step One- UNCOVER OPPORTUNITIES - Recap

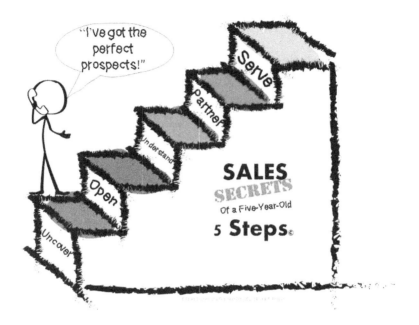

- Seek people who have problems that you, your product or service can solve.
- Have an optimistic and enthusiastic approach to prospecting.
- Don't be lazy. Get up early and make prospecting a priority.
- Be relentless. Don't be deterred because the work is hard. Nothing good is easy.
- Set aggressive goals and track your progress daily.
- Know your numbers, ratios and where your skill gaps are, then work to improve them.
- Embrace technology. Use CRMs and SFAs, along with social media, to drive efficient and effective prospecting.
- Let everyone know what you do and how they can help.
- Be loud so you can be heard above the noise. Market yourself and grow your personal brand.
- Be a great storyteller so you can relate to more prospects.
- Network—build a referral list and ask for referrals.

- Set aside time to prospect and do it daily so you don't get behind.
- Do your homework. Gather plenty of data, but do it quickly and efficiently.
- Be fearless on the phone. Learn to love the challenge and the process.
- Work with the gatekeeper and ask for the right way to set appointments.
- Know that all prospects care about FIP, but more importantly, be able to articulate how your products can positively impact FIP.
- Have a value proposition that is concise, gets attention and adds value.
- Be prepared for any situation you may encounter while prospecting.
- Ask a lot of questions. Be naturally curious.
- Don't overthink—just go for it! You add value, so just go out believing that!
- Write handwritten cards as follow up to prospects you can't get into.
- Follow up diligently as it will often take five to eight contacts with a prospect before they will meet with you.
- Remember to have fun!

Let's Get This Party Started

STEP 2: OPENING A SALES CALL

"I came here to have a good time." – Brendin (age 5)

While kids are sometimes reluctant to start something new, once they become comfortable with the process—even when new people are introduced to the process—they are more concerned with having a good time than about anything else. I used to help my children become more familiar with a new scenario by letting them know that they needed to help people.

People (kids especially) naturally want to help people. Opening a sales call should be no different; the focus should be on a good time for you and the prospect or client while *helping* THEM. And regardless of how many times you have met with a prospect or client, you must open the sales call each time you meet with them. Through this, you should get very comfortable with opening a sales call. In this step, you will learn how to properly open a sales call.

"That's a really cool painting." – Kids notice things and build rapport!

Kids seem to notice everything and aren't shy about asking questions. When my oldest daughter was about ten, I took her along to my doctor's appointment and I remember how she looked around at all of the paintings on the waiting room wall. She was genuinely curious and even asked the nurse which one she liked best.

When we got to the exam room and the doctor came in, before I could even greet the doctor, my daughter smiled and said, "I love all of the paintings in your office and noticed your name on them. Did you paint all of those?"

The doctor smiled and said, "Yes I did. Which one is your favorite?" Now, I had been to that doctor's office dozens of times and spent hours there and had never noticed what took a ten-year-old three minutes to notice. She then used what she noticed to build rapport with an adult she had never met.

Building rapport on a sales call is crucial and over the years, I have read about how sales professionals should use things in the prospect's office to ask questions about and build rapport. I will caution you, however, that this is an old and common practice used without a lot of success for one reason or another.

In one instance, I was on a first meeting with a prospect and asked him if he caught the fish he had hanging on the wall. He looked me right in the face and said, "Nope. I keep it up there to see how many stupid salespeople will ask about it."

What I learned on that sales call is that you must be sincere and not just take the easy way to build rapport. If you carefully read the section on uncovering opportunity, you should have already visited the prospect's website, LinkedIn profile and searched for details about them online so you have a baseline of things to ask about. You can look for obvious commonalities like the same college attended, hometown, or similar work history, but I would suggest looking for a more personal connection like those involving charity or community involvement, which will help establish rapport in a faster and more meaningful manner.

"I just want to help!" – Kids love to help and have a pure intent!

When my kids were young, no matter what I was cooking, they were always willing to help. They didn't care that they didn't know how to do something or that they may make a huge mess, causing more work than if they didn't help. Their intent was pure, and they only wanted to help. That made me overlook the fact that by them helping, it often took more time or created a bigger mess. People are naturally more inclined to buy in and to even be more forgiving if something goes wrong if they feel that the intent of the other person wanting to help is pure. As a sales professional, you must develop a sincere, pure desire to help others. If you are only in sales for money and yourself, you will never be successful long-term. You must have a client-focused approach, centered around helping and serving them, and by that, you will be handsomely and consistently rewarded.

"I am excited to be here." – Kids get excited!

I love seeing how genuinely excited kids get when they are introduced to someone or something new, and how that excitement almost doubles when they believe they can help. Opening a sales call sets the stage for the entire meeting and the prospect or client should feel that genuine excitement and your desire to help them. I'm not saying to be over the top or to talk loudly, as these things aren't needed to show sincere excitement. Sincere excitement is the mindset that you are happily there to help someone, and the excitement may be shown as something as simple as a confident handshake and a smile.

Kids are also very prideful in their work and believe that they are making a difference. Prospects can see and feel pride in someone. They can tell whether someone's intentions to help are pure and will respond accordingly.

This is a good time to restate your value proposition, especially if there is anyone new in the room who hasn't heard why it is important that you are there that day.

"I want you to meet the best mom in the whole world." – Kids know that introductions are important!

I can remember trying to explain in greater detail who I am or what I did to new people we would meet after my kids would give me perhaps the most glowing introduction ever. They would say things like, "I want to introduce the best dad ever. He is so strong; he writes books and his picture is on Google and everything."

As flattering as these grand introductions were, I knew my kids were on to something when it came to introductions that help set a stage and show the value of a person who is present. How many times have you been introduced in a sales call and been given no hype—no background on who you are, what you specialize in or why you are there on that call?

The trend of team selling is only growing, and sales professionals aren't investing enough time on developing better team-selling skills, in my opinion. Introductions are the start of building great team-selling sales calls. You don't have to use the same degree of hype that my kids used, but try to build value even with the introductions instead of introducing your manager to the prospect by saying something like, "This is Kristen. She is my boss and wanted to come out and meet you, as well."

Try introducing them more like this: "This is Kristen. She is responsible for leading the entire sales team I work on and has been with the company for seven years. The reason I decided to bring her today is because of her expertise in solving problems for clients in your same industry. I wanted to make the most of our time today, so I brought as much expertise as I could."

The fact that the second introduction tells a bit more story, background and *purpose* for bringing someone else on the call, increases the prospect's buy-in.

"This trip to the amusement park just won't be as great if we don't get cotton candy and ride the rollercoaster." – Kids set objectives!

As a kid, going to the amusement park wasn't a *success* if we didn't get to eat cotton candy and ride the rollercoaster at least twice. What I realize now that I didn't realize then is that as kids, we set objectives to gauge the fun we expected to have. These were tangible and measurable objectives. If we didn't eat cotton candy, we weren't successful.

As a sales professional, how do you know if you have run a successful sales call? Are you setting measurable objectives that let you know if/when you have reached success?

Most sales pros I have coached over the years say to never just tell me that a sales call was "great" without letting me know exactly what objectives were met that led you to think it was "great." In other words, "great" is subjective, meaning many different things to different people. For one person, "great" might just mean that the prospect didn't kick them out of the office, whereas to another, "great" means they closed the sale.

It's important to note that each sales call should have a different set of objectives, too. For instance, setting the objective of closing the sale may not be the best objective if it is your first meeting with the prospect and you know you have at least a sixty-day sales cycle.

You should also have multiple objectives and back-up objectives in case the first set of objectives can't be reached because the timing isn't right, or the right people aren't present, etc. And depending on what industry you serve, your sales cycle could be years instead of weeks or months and therefore your objectives will be different and probably less aggressive than, say, someone with a thirty-day sales cycle.

The important thing to know is that regardless of how aggressive the objective is, it must be measurable. You must know if and when the objective has been reached.

One of the best ways to achieve this is to use action words to set the objective, like *measure, design, determine, decide, discover, implement, sign off on, introduce, agree on,* etc. Focus on action words that fit the vertical market and product suite you sell. This way, you will know how to prepare for and approach the sales call—what questions to ask, whom to invite, and so on.

And when you are asked if the sales call was a success, you will only need to reflect on if the objectives were met to decide whether success (or at least progress) was achieved. Some good first meeting objectives may sound like this: "Determine if a need exists. Uncover the decision-making process. Determine the prospect's timeline. Tell my high-level story of why they should consider me, my company and product."

Objectives will be your gauge of sales-call success and you should design them to move the sale forward with each call.

"I don't want to be the same as everyone else." – Kids know that differentiation is key!

When my oldest son was about seven, he never wanted to dress like the other kids. He preferred bright colors or mis-matched shoes. When I asked him why, he just said, "I don't want to be the same as the other kids."

When opening a sales call, you should strive to differentiate yourself so you aren't seen as the same as others, too. You don't have to wear bright colors or mis-matched shoes. These days, differentiation can start by simply showing up early for your appointment, dressing professionally and being well groomed. But when the playing field is equal regarding the basics, you can stand out by producing and using a written agenda. Since so few salespeople use written agendas, even when they are mandated by the company they work for, producing and using one can really help you stand out in a positive way. Written agendas serve many purposes, so let's dig a little deeper into what else they can do and how to effectively build and use one.

"I always eat breakfast at 7 a.m." – Kids are structured and have agendas!

Once, I woke my kids up earlier than usual to get them ready and fed so we could get on the road for our family vacation. I remember my daughter saying, "But Daddy, we don't eat right now. We eat breakfast at 7." Kids are creatures of habit for a reason.

Since we were in utero, we were introduced to structure. We ate at a certain time, slept at a certain time, and so on. After we are born, our parents get us on a structure as quickly as possible. They feed us, bathe us and put us to bed a certain time and we tend to stay on a similar type of structure our entire life.

Humans are actually wired to perform better when there is structure. We have even learned this from survivors who were rescued from situations like being stranded on a deserted island. Many found ways to count the passing days, eat at a certain time and continue a routine of structure, even without any semblance of society.

Since we are hardwired to have structure in our lives, why would we want to attempt a sales call without structure? Written agendas give us the proper structure needed to have productive meetings. The agenda also shows the prospect that you respect the time that has been given for the meeting and that you intend to use the time wisely.

Agendas should always contain several things. The first is the client company name and time, date and location of the meeting, along with the attendees' names, both your team and theirs. The agenda should also carefully outline the meeting parts, roles and goals of the attendees, along with a list of topics (THAT SUPPORT THE OBJECTIVE OF THE SALES CALL) and the timeline for each. Do not add any agenda items that do not help meet the meeting objective. These are time wasters and will elongate your sales process.

Here is a sample of what an agenda might look like. You can download this template and others like it at www.mikealmorgan.com.

			MEETING AGENDA	
YOUR COMPANY NAME/LOGO			Date: Time:	
			Location:	
			Webinar/Dial-in Information:	

Attendees (YOUR COMPANY NAME) Names and Titles

Attendees (PROSPECT COMPANY NAME) Names and Titles

Objective of this meeting:

Time Allotted	Topic	Presenter	Goal	Questions or Action Item
10 Minutes	Introductions	All	Understand the roles, goals and value each person brings	
10 Minutes	Topic Here	Presenter name Here	Goal of covering topic	Outstanding things that need clarification, etc.

Follow Up Notes:

Next Steps (Prospect Company) Names and Responsibilities

Next Steps (Your Company) Names and Responsibilities

Next Meeting Date:

Once the agenda has been created, email it to the prospect, asking if anything should be added or removed. This will differentiate you to an even greater degree and allow you to get buy-in from the prospect.

It also shows the prospect that you are vested—and investing—in the meeting. You can also include any additional digital supporting documentation or links to product videos, etc., that will enhance the discussion you want to have, if applicable.

Now that you have built your agenda and shared it with the prospect, you must properly position and use it if you want to get the most out of it. When you pull the agenda out of your bag, don't just hand it out and say, "Here are some things we can go over today."

Take the time to pass the agendas out to everyone attending and discuss the high-level importance of each topic. And then use it to guide you through the sales call, getting you closer to meeting the objective. If the meeting begins to go in directions that you don't want it to go, use the agenda to ask questions about the next topic to steer the meeting back where it was designed to go.

After skillfully positioning the agenda, let the prospect know how you can impact them and their business, then carefully set the stage and prepare the prospect for how the meeting will go, specifically regarding all of the questions you will ask. Explain that the more open they are with you, the more you will learn and be able to help.

I say to *carefully* set the stage because some prospects are reluctant to open up either out of ignorance or blindness to what is going on in their own business, or out of fear that something painful will be uncovered that they will need to deal with through this "interrogation." Keep in mind that we seek business problems like a doctor screens for health issues— what you find early will cost a person significantly less if/when treated now than if discovered/treated later.

Opening a sales call sets the stage and creates the foundation you will sell on. Make sure it is a great foundation.

Step Two– OPENING A SALES CALL– Recap

- Notice the right things so you can build good rapport.
- Have honest intent to help people – be in sales for the right reason.
- Be excited. Excitement will transfer to the prospect.
- Focus on making great introductions built on value and purpose.
- Set strong meeting objectives so you can move sales further, faster.
- Frame sales calls properly with a written agenda, showing the prospect that you have prepared and that you value the time being invested.
- Send the agenda prior to the call and adjust it accordingly based on what the prospect thinks is important.
- Use the agenda to keep the meeting on track and meet your objective.
- Set the proper stage to ask questions so the prospect understands why they are being asked questions and feels more comfortable about sharing information.

Oh, I get it!

STEP 3: UNDERSTANDING PROSPECTS

"Why?" —Skyler (age 5) and every kid, ever

In this step, you will get a sense of how kids and successful sales professionals are better prepared to sell because of the knowledge they gain through asking great questions, listening and organizing. You will learn how to uncover business needs and problems and to create urgency by asking strategic questions. I will then cover how to organize what you learn through proper sales funnel management.

"I hear you!" – Kids can be very attentive listeners!

When I was young, my family didn't have a lot of money, so summers were spent at the local library instead of on cruise ships or sandy beaches. I still remember spending hours reading hundreds of books. I loved using books to escape to a sandy beach, if only in my mind. While I loved reading, my favorite part of spending time at the library was when the librarian gathered the kids to read us a story. We all sat with our legs crossed, so quiet and attentive, in anticipation of that day's story. We listened and hung on every single word as the story carried us far away from that old library.

Asking questions is only 50% of the skills needed to truly understand prospects and clients. To really understand, you must be able to ask great questions and have the ability to *listen.*

There several ways to listen, including passive, empathetic, reflective and active listing. Actively listening is what is needed in sales, as it requires the listener to not only concentrate on what the speaker is saying, but to fully understand, remember and respond when appropriate.

Speak in such a way that others love to listen to you. Listen in such a way that others love to speak to you. - Zig Ziglar

---

For a sales professional, actively listening is paramount in building good relationships with both prospects and clients. It will also prove helpful when preparing presentations and proposals on what prospects and clients are really looking for. Don't ever assume—if you don't listen, you won't know.

A sales professional who can speak six languages, isn't as impressive as a sales professional who can <u>listen</u> in one. - Unknown

---

Here are some things you can do to become a more active listener:

- ✓ Don't multitask or just wait for your turn to talk. Put 100% of your focus on the speaker, giving full and undivided attention.

- ✓ Don't assume; go into the conversation as if you know nothing about the person or topic.

- ✓ Encourage the conversation along by asking open-ended questions like, "Tell me more about that?" or "Who else could that impact?"

- ✓ Use body language to show your interest. Lean in, nod and give verbal and non-verbal cues that show you are engaged.

- ✓ Check for understanding by asking re-cap questions like, "If I understand you correctly, you are saying that . . .?"

- ✓ Listen for more than what is being said. Actively listening means listening for an entire message, including a theme or feelings behind the actual words being said.

"What is that? Who put it there? When did it get there? Where did it come from? WHY is it there?" – Kids are expert question askers!

Why is the sky blue? Why is water wet? How do birds fly? The list goes on and on. One of the most underrated sales skills in the world is the one that kids seem to have mastered hands down—the skill of asking questions. While it can be frustrating at times to be peppered with questions by a young child, most people don't lose patience when kids are asking a million questions, because of a kid's natural curiosity and honest intent.

Kids do a great job of asking a lot of "what, when and how" questions. But kids truly shine in asking the one type of question that stimulates the mind more than any other, and is ironically the one we stop asking as we get older: the "why" question.

As a sales professional, you should prepare for sales calls by practicing all question types. Script them out and carry a list of great questions you can ask prospects and clients. I even carried a list of questions that I could ask a CEO or COO if given the opportunity, because I learned a long time ago that we are judged much more on the questions we ask than the answers we give. I found I could captivate a CEO by asking him or her, "What is the single most important thing that all employees at your company should know, and why?" much more than I could by stating an elevator pitch that told them about me or my product.

An elevator pitch tells the prospect how important you are.

A sincere question lets the prospect know how important they are.

Sharpen your questioning skills and learn to ask everything about each question type. Your objective with your questioning model while on a sales call is to build a very <u>clear and complete understanding of your prospect and everything about their business, goals and problems.</u> Specifically, *you are seeking problems* that your product or service can satisfy—but don't start selling just yet. You are merely in problem-seeking and information-gathering mode at this point. The time to sell will come later. Right now, focus on building that clear and complete picture as you will more than likely use all the data you gather when building your presentation and/or proposal.

I have been known to start a sales call with a prospect I have never met with, using this question: "Thank you for taking this time with me today. May I ask what the number one reason you agreed to meet with me today is?" Pay close attention to the response as usually you will learn their biggest problem that they believe you could help them with. Write down the response and ask follow-up questions around that response, as you will use this information later. At worst, you learn what you did that worked to get the appointment and you can double down on that tactic going forward. In some cases, they may have just agreed to meet with you due to your persistence and follow up.

Before you begin what may be mistaken as an interrogation, it's important that you set the stage! After that question, as mentioned at the end of the chapter on opening the sales call, before you start with the what, who, when, where, how and why question model, make sure that you explain to the prospect that you'd like to ask them a series of questions that may seem irrelevant at first, but that you promise that the questions will help you fully understand their unique situation.

Start with **WHAT** questions: What do you do you here? What does the company do to make money? What are the biggest business problems you have here? What is the most expensive business problem you face here? What is the most frustrating business problem you have? What compliance concerns have you dealt with? What can you tell me about your company that only someone who works here would know? Or any other relevant "what" questions you can think of that will help you open more of a sales dialog.

You can even expand to "what if" questions. These are possibility questions, like: What if you were to expand business operations too prematurely? What if your office lost all communications? What if they made you CEO tomorrow—what would you do first? And so on.

Move on to **WHO** questions: Who owns the problems? Who works here? Who are your clients? Who are your competitors? Who reports to whom? Who will benefit most from solving X? Keep going with *natural* curiosity until you have exhausted the WHO questions.

WHEN questions:
· When do these problems occur?
· When is your fiscal year-end?
· When is payroll?
· When do people report to work?
· When do you compete paperwork? Or any other relevant "when" questions you can think of that will help you open more of a sales dialog or discover additional business problems.

WHERE questions:
· Where do these problems happen?
· Where all do you do business?
· Where are you looking to expand?
· Where do you overlap with your competitors? Or any other relevant "where" questions you can think of that will help you open more of a sales dialog or discover additional business problems.

HOW questions:
- How do you determine what good service is?
- How do you like to be handled as a client?
- How was the current solution chosen?
- How do you like for someone to follow up with you?

And **WHY** questions, which are great follow-up questions to the other question types, to help paint a more clear and complete picture.
- Why is that the case?
- Why do you feel that way?
- Why is it important? Etc. "Why" questions are critical because they typically evoke feelings and help you understand the feelings behind the answers you are getting.

For more specific questions, you should add what you've learned from your homework and couple that with your questions. For example, say you read on the company website that the company you are meeting with sells pipes and valves. You may ask the client, "I saw that you specialize in selling pipes and valves. Are those your only revenue streams or do you also specialize in anything else?" Or you may use a related industry statistic you've learned and couple that with a question that will open a sales dialog for your product or service. If you sold human resource services or safety products, for example, you might ask, "I read a statistic that 66% of companies in your industry have one to two work-related injuries each month. Does your company experience that many work-related injuries?"

It is also important to balance your questions between open-ended questions (those that call for speculation or opinion) and closed questions (yes or no questions or those with a specific, factual answer), with the emphasis being on the former. Open-ended questions allow the prospect to expound on the details, giving you more information and ability to fully understand the situation.

Closed questions have a purpose and serve in narrowing down or clarifying a vague response. Balance is the key. With only open-ended questions, your sales call might last for several hours. With only closed-ended questions, you might have to ask 40 questions to get a clear answer. However, a slight imbalance of open and closed probes may be helpful with prospects who are not very forthcoming. In that case, you will want to start with an open-ended question and then follow up with closed ones.

Here is an example:

Me: "What is the biggest problem you face here?" (OPEN)
Prospect: "Overtime."
Me: "What about overtime is the problem?" (CLOSED)
Prospect: "It costs us a fortune."
Me: "Who has the overtime?" (CLOSED)
Prospect: "Our drivers."
Me: "When and where primarily does the overtime happen and how is the time worked captured?" (CLOSED)
Me: "And why do you feel like there is so much overtime? Is it a lack of staff or ineffective or inefficient staff?" (OPEN)

This what, who, when, where, how and why question line-up gets the prospect to give me very specific details about the overtime problem they face. You will be able to gather a lot of information if you follow this questioning model, but you still have some big gaps to fill because you still don't know how, when or why they make decisions. That is where BART comes in.

Being naturally curious and asking qustions has a side effect of making the prospect feel valued, listened to and important.

"Do you know B.A.R.T?" – Kids keep asking questions!

Kids keep asking questions even when it seems like they have all the answers they could possibly need. Additional questions kids like to ask are things like why things are the way they are, who is in charge, how much money people have and what time it is.

These all happen to be the perfect questions to qualify a prospect. You see, prospects must be properly qualified if you are going to sell them anything. And to keep the process as simple as possible, BART is one of only three acronyms I use in this program to help organize a system for obtaining information.

BART stands for:

Buying Criteria | Authority | Resources | Timeline

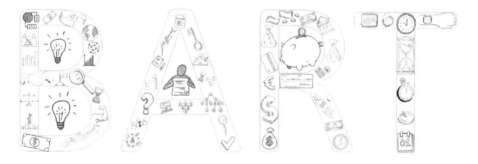

Let's start with the **B** for buying criteria. This simply means why a prospect would choose a product and what criteria they have used in the past to evaluate and make decisions on similar products. Each step of BART is important, and the reason this step is important is because without getting this information, you will be left guessing at what they most want out of a product or service and ultimately why they would choose one over another.

In sales, you must know what the buying criteria is and why, and in what priority order, so you can build your presentation accordingly.

We can learn a lot about this by asking about why the current system was chosen. In some cases, there is nothing currently in place.

Either way, you should ask about ideal, preferred outcomes. You also can't assume that because something is important to the prospect that it is a buying criteria. For instance, a prospect might tell you that safety is important when selecting a particular line of car, but when asked more specifically about why they will select a particular car, they will tell you things like fuel economy or leg room. That is because they believe that safety is standard in that entire line of vehicles.

To get more information about the buying criteria, ask questions like:
- What is the ideal outcome you are looking for and what will this outcome do for your business?
- Why was the current system chosen and has anything changed since these considerations were most important?
- What criteria will you use to evaluate the company that will provide the solution to you?
- What will you use to evaluate the ideal company representative you will choose to represent this solution?

The biggest priority for you that you must have in a solution is the "what." Now, get the prospect to rank these *in priority order* so you can get a better understanding of the relative importance of each.

But who is really making decisions? Let's ask about the **A**, for authority. Most salespeople's attempts to identify the prospect's decision-making process fail miserably because they tend to overthink the hell out of it and ask questions like, "Who besides yourself makes important decisions here regarding (whatever they sell)?" The problem with this question is that it paints the prospect into a corner and ego will usually speak up on behalf of the prospect and the answer is usually a resounding, "ME! I make all important decisions about, well, *everything* around here!"

This will become an issue later in your buying cycle when the deal stalls and you try to get answers from this prospect because you think he or she is stalling on the decision, when in reality someone else altogether is the decision maker. So, how do you get the prospect to put their guard down and answer truthfully, but still keep their dignity intact?

Let's test your ability to think through this without overthinking: **What is the best question you could possibly ask to determine the prospect's decision-making process?**

You passed if you said, "Can you please tell me about your decision-making process?"

That is the best question you can ask to determine the process! This allows the prospect to tell you all about the process and perhaps what role they play, etc. In some cases, you can turn the written agenda over and have the prospect sketch out the process right there, so you also get a visual of how it works.

You can then ask if it is appropriate to invite some of the people they mention in the process to attend some of the later meetings you will schedule, so they can hear directly from you, be able to ask you questions directly, etc. Make sure you ask follow-up questions about what is important to the other people who will be involved in that process. You don't want to assume that just because a CFO is involved, they only care about cost. Ask follow-up questions to be sure.

But can they afford what you have to offer? The **R** is for resources!

Establishing whether the prospect has the appropriate resources is so important because without all of the right resources, the deal could stall or fall out altogether. Keeping in mind that finances can be a delicate subject, when is the right time to discuss money, credit or other resources the prospect will need to make a purchase?

It is better to find out early on, even if it is not the answer you want, so you can move on to another prospect that does have the appropriate resources rather than wasting time with ones that don't. I was told years ago that in sales, you want to close fast or lose fast! It made more sense the more years I spent in sales, as so many salespeople stay hung up on what could be if things were different. If things aren't right, move on to a follow-up plan, and maybe the prospect's circumstances will change. At that point, you can re-engage. Until then, find prospects that have the right resources.

A good way to determine resources is to ask questions like:
- What can you tell me about the budget that has been allocated for this project?
- Just so I better understand all elements of how you typically do business, how do you typically pay for these types of services with other partners? Is it with a purchase order, check, corporate credit card or other form of payment?
- When you have made purchases for these types of services in the past, what is the typical approval process for this level of purchase?

Now, when will all of this take place? The **T** for timeline will tell us!

Timeline questions aren't difficult to ask. Determining the prospect's timeline can still be tricky, however. Some deals are straightforward. You are able to positively satisfy all aspects of BART and they seem like they want to move quickly, and then . . . nothing.

This is the point where salespeople use a bunch of black-op, military lingo to describe the situation. They will say things like, "I don't know what happened to my deal—they went radio silent on me." Or, "The guy is MIA. I can't find him anywhere." One of my favorites is, "My prospect ghosted me!"

When we get "ghosted"—when the prospect seems to disappear—it is typically because there was a breakdown in one part or another of BART. Something changed in the prospect organization regarding the buying criteria. The need to change could have become less urgent due to several factors. Their current product/system began working correctly, or was more aggressively priced by the incumbent provider, or perhaps the support improved. This is why the steps in BART should be followed carefully and the questions asked with care.

For timeline questions, you can begin with simple, straightforward ones like:

- How soon would you like to begin seeing (whatever benefit your product will provide)?
- When do you plan on implementing a new (whatever product you sell)?

Complete your timeline questions by asking a follow-up question that will allow you to determine what things could impact the timeline, like:

- Do you anticipate anything that would disrupt the timeline you have given me—things like mergers, acquisitions, layoffs, changes in company structure, budget constraints, or other issues?

Once you have firm, positive answers to all four parts of BART, congratulations! You now have a qualified prospect. This means that the prospect at least has a need and the overall ability to fill that need.

But what happens when there are no business problems to solve? When there are no needs to fill, you must use the acronym that I named SIIR to find them!

"Yes, SIIR." – Kids use "manners" to find business problems!

Kids are great at creating a need, using "what if" and "why" questions with precision and making an idea seem like it was yours all along!

Some years ago, my oldest daughter asked me if I was thinking about taking a vacation.

I said, "Well, we took one last summer and I am pretty busy at work, so no, I hadn't really considered taking one right now." She immediately went into SIIR questions.

HER: "Dad, tell me about the situation at work. Sounds stressful!"

ME: "Yeah, it's pretty stressful. We are always looking for more sales!"

HER: "Oh no! What issues does that cause with your blood pressure when you get stressed out?" *(Using information she already has, coupled with a question.)*

ME: "Well, it's not great. If my blood pressure gets out of whack, I could get sick like I did before and have to slow down a bit."

HER: "Oh yeah, sounds like it could impact your work and your health if your blood pressure got too high. Could that cost you money if it did?"

ME: "Yes, sweetie, I guess it could cost Dad quite a bit if I was actually forced to take off of work because of my blood pressure."

HER: "I wish there was a short cruise we could take! I bet you could lower your blood pressure and get some much-needed rest and not have to take a longer time off like if you got sick. The cruise pays for itself almost right away."

SOLD! But who am I kidding? It doesn't take much arm twisting for me to agree to take a cruise! What my daughter used is called a Socratic question model.

While I am not in the habit of quoting from Wikipedia, I found this explanation of Socratic questions to be written quite well, so I thought I'd share: (3)

> Socratic questioning was named after Socrates, who is thought to have lived c. 470 BCE–c. 399 BCE. Socrates utilized an educational method that focused on discovering answers by asking questions from his students. According to Plato, Socrates believed that "the disciplined practice of thoughtful questioning enables the scholar/student to examine ideas and be able to determine the validity of those ideas." Plato, a student of Socrates, described this rigorous method of teaching to explain that the teacher assumes an ignorant mindset in order to compel the student to assume the highest level of knowledge.

This method of questioning is extremely compelling in sales when you need to create a need, or even a sense of urgency in what seems to be the absence of one. I framed it with the acronym of SIIR to make it as simple as possible for you to remember and use. Keep in mind that each question builds on the previous one, so each of the Situation, Issues, Impacts and Recommendation questions should be used in this order.

Situation Questions. Discover what the current situation is by asking direct questions about the status of the prospect's current situation or circumstances:

- "Can you tell me what you are currently doing about X?"
- "What is the status of your X?"
- "Can you walk me through a day in the life of X?"

Issue Questions. Ask questions to determine what issues exist within the current situation:

- "What issues do you have with X?"
- "Could the results be better?"
- "Would you change anything about how this is currently running?"

You can also use any information you have previously uncovered to aid in these questions:

- "Based on the rising cost of fuel, what issues do you foresee coming up with this situation?"

Impact Questions. Here you want to dig into the *hard costs* or other "pain" associated with the issues you have just uncovered. Write down these tangible and intangible impacts. Keep in mind that for some prospects, the intangible pain—if great enough—could move them to make a decision to buy from you, even if your product costs more than your competitor's. These questions include the following:

- "How much does that issue cost you when it happens?"
- "How often does it happen?"
- "What impact will this issue have on budget?" (Tangible)
- "How frustrating is it when this happens? (Intangible)
- "How will this impact your plans of X?"
- "How has this impacted your department/job?"

Recommendation Questions. The recommendation question requires a more subtle approach so that the prospect thinks the result is their idea. You do this by using one of those "If there was only a way," or "What do you recommend?" sort of questions:
- "What type of solution do you think could solve this type of concern?"
- "What do you think your competitors do when they face a similar concern?"

Now that you have led the prospect down a path of self-discovery and have them really thinking about what could be—or perhaps thinking about how bad their situation really is, as well as how much it is costing them to do business the way they are, etc.—it is important to capture as many of these problems as you can. Review the list you have uncovered and ask the prospect to help you by prioritizing the challenges they face so you know where to put your focus, first.

"I pick toys up in this order: big ones first, then small ones!"
– Kids can be great at classifying and organizing!

Kids love puzzles and challenging toys that force them to think. I walked into my kids' room one time to find them picking up toys, and after I got over my initial shock that they were doing this, I saw that they also were challenging each other to pick up toys in alphabetical order by first name of the toy. Later that day they did it again, this time by size. That night, just before bed, they picked up once more, and this time they did it in order of which toy was their favorite, from most to least favorite.

When it comes to understanding prospects and clients, you must tap into the creativity and diligence of organizing that kids often demonstrate. Organizing the data you've collected is important not only so you better understand the needs, priorities of needs and details of the prospect, but so you can use it later in the sales process to successfully convert the prospect into a client.

A sales funnel (or pipeline, as it is sometimes called), is the very best way to organize the information and status of the opportunities you uncover from your prospects and clients as they move through the sales cycle. You should set aside time every day to manage sales funnels, as this is the lifeblood of any great sales professional. Update each opportunity with what happened that day, and if nothing happened with that opportunity that day, follow up with it to attempt to move it forward. While you may not get to all of the opportunities in your funnel each day, this practice will have you touching more than if you don't use this practice.

A funnel, used properly, is a sales enablement tool. Used improperly, it is a source of frustration, extra work and false hope.

Your company might already have funnel standards in place, in which case you should be sure to use those, but you should still pay attention here as you may want to incorporate some of this methodology into what you currently use. The funnel I use maintains a simple flow, regardless of the complexity of the product I sell. The funnel serves as a representation of the sales process where opportunities live in various stages. The funnel I will teach you about here is based on working through opportunities on a monthly basis, bringing opportunities from about 120 days from closing, through a 90- and 60-day process, into a 30-day window to close, which is how most companies are set up to compensate outside sales professionals.

The sales funnel also begins to explain why I refer to the prospect as *prospect* instead of *client*, as they are only a client after they have gone through the sales funnel and have paid you or are in the process of paying. One other thing to point out on that note is that the sales funnel should be used to track individual *opportunities*, not companies. Meaning, if you sell different products or the same product to different departments within a single company, you may close the account by closing an initial sale, turning them from prospect to client, but still have many more individual opportunities in the sales funnel. Each opportunity is treated separately, and can live in different stages of the funnel, regardless of which company they are associated with.

Each stage has certain criteria or a set of milestones that must be met for an opportunity to be properly classified in that stage. Opportunities then must meet a new set of milestones in order to progress through the funnel. The funnel is a great representation of a sales cycle because, for the most part, like a funnel, what you put in comes out, just at a slower rate. However, if you don't carefully follow each step I have outlined (and sometimes even if you do), the funnel can turn into a very porous sieve, leaking opportunities everywhere.

That is why it is critical that you use the stages of the funnel and update your progress made on your active opportunities daily so that the funnel remains **FULL, FACTUAL and FLOWING**!

One important thing to note is that the funnel should always contain two ingredients: honesty and accuracy. These are so important because of the adage "garbage in, garbage out." You need a true reflection of the opportunities you are working, so never add opportunities just to make yourself feel better about having something in the funnel.

If you build your funnel the right way, it will be a reliable source of information and aid you in closing more sales. However, if you decide to fill your funnel with lies and false deals, your funnel will turn into a burden, a cause of extra work and frustration instead of the sales enablement tool it is designed to be.

Here is the graphic representation of the sale funnel I've always used that includes the stages, statistics and targets you should strive for in each stage.

I'll explain the funnel stages and the milestones that must be met that qualify an opportunity to be classified in each stage and when it is appropriate to move it to the next stage.

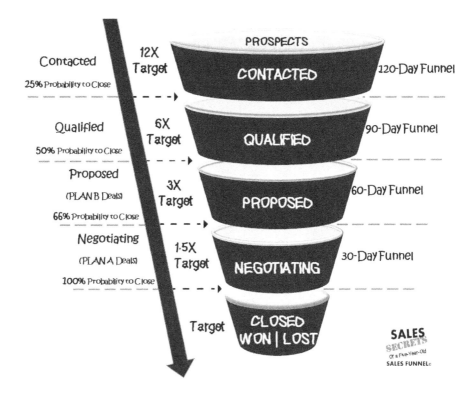

Always keep your funnel FULL, FACTUAL AND FLOWING!

CONTACTED: Also referred to as your **120-day funnel**.

Based on research or other means, you *think* they have a problem that you can solve.

The probability of closing an opportunity at this stage of the sales cycle is approximately 25%. Because of that low probability, you should have ten times the number of opportunities you need to close in this stage of the funnel. These opportunities, if you work them diligently, will progress to the later stages of the funnel, but at varying speeds. Some will progress quickly, while others will stall for months or even years, depending on the prospect's sense of urgency. This is because this is an early stage and the fallout potential in this (and subsequent stages of the funnel) is *significant* at this point.

In the Contacted stage, from your homework or a conversation with the prospect, you know the prospect has a problem that you can solve. **No timeline has been established.**

Milestones that must be met in order to place an opportunity in this stage:
- You have done homework on the prospect and know at least three things about the prospect.
- The prospect at least agrees to speak with you about their business.
- You have told them your value proposition.
- A virtual or in-person meeting has been scheduled.

The opportunity will stay here in the Contacted stage until the following milestones are met. Once they are, the opportunity can be then moved to the Qualified stage.
- A virtual or in-person meeting has taken place.
- The prospect willingly shares information with you.
- The prospect meets all of the BART criteria.
- You have identified at least one business problem and you've confirmed that your product or service can solve that problem.
- At least a loose timeline has been established.
- You have *not* delivered a formal quote or proposal.

QUALIFIED: Also referred to as your **90-day funnel**.
**The prospect knows they have a problem and is willing to explore fixing
it. Both you *and* the prospect have the capacity to fix the problem.**

The probability of closing an opportunity at this stage of the sales cycle
is 50%, so you should have at least six times the number of opportunities
you need to close in this stage of the funnel, because again, these
opportunities will progress at varying paces through the funnel. And, just
because the prospect has a problem and you can solve it, doesn't mean
they will let you. This is still an early funnel stage and losing the
opportunity in this stage of the funnel (and subsequent stages) is a risk
at this point.

In the Qualified stage, you have met with the prospect, and they meet all
of the BART criteria. There is mutual interest in solving the prospect's
problem; both parties are interested in moving forward.

**Milestones that must be met in order to place an opportunity in this
stage:**
- A virtual or in-person meeting has taken place.
- The prospect willingly shares information with you.
- The prospect meets all of the BART criteria.
- You have identified at least one business problem and you've
  confirmed that your product or service can solve that problem.
- You have *not* delivered a formal quote or proposal.
- At least a loose timeline has been established that you believe would
  allow the opportunity to be closed within a 90-day window.
- The prospect agrees to at least explore solving the problem.

**The opportunity will stay here in the Qualified stage until the following
milestones are met. Once they are, the opportunity can be then moved
to the Proposed stage.**
- A formal proposal or quote has been delivered to the prospect.
- A formal presentation and technical demonstration (if applicable)
  have been presented to the prospect.
- You have answered any outstanding questions the prospect has.

PROPOSED: Also referred to as your **60-day funnel**.
You have met with, presented and proposed your solution to their problem.

Since the prospect has agreed to review your proposal, the probability of closing an opportunity at this stage of the sales cycle is 66%. Therefore, you should still have at least three times the opportunities you need to close in this stage of the funnel. Even with this being a later stage of the funnel, there is still some risk of losing the opportunity. The primary reason the probability to close is set at 66% at this point is that you are now discussing price, terms and conditions of purchasing.

Here is where the rule of thirds for funnel management is a factor. This formula has proven to be extremely accurate in my experience for the *Proposed* stage of the funnel, and explains why I said you should have at least three times the number of opportunities you need in this stage . Keep in mind that you must follow all of the steps and have a truly qualified opportunity for the formula to be accurate.

This formula simply states that for opportunities in the Qualified stage:

- ⊘ 1/3 of proposed opportunities will close when you anticipate they will.

- ⊘ 1/3 of proposed opportunities will close at a date later than you anticipate.

- ⊘ 1/3 of proposed opportunities will never close, and will be lost forever.

In the Proposed stage, you have met with the prospect and delivered a formal proposal or quote for the prospect to review.

Always deliver the formal quote or proposal in person, if possible. You want to be able to read body language and gauge nonverbal cues about their satisfaction when first seeing your proposal.

The opportunities in this stage should serve as your backup or **"plan B deals,"** meaning that most are not fully ready to close but that a catalyst like a promotion or other sales tactic could possibly be deployed to bring this opportunity to close sooner.

Milestones that must be met in order to place an opportunity in this stage:
- o A formal proposal or quote has been delivered to the prospect.
- o A formal presentation and technical demonstration (if applicable) have been presented to the prospect.
- o You have answered any outstanding questions the prospect has.
- o The timeline of the prospect would allow the opportunity to be closed within a 60-day window.

The opportunity will stay here in the Proposed stage until the following milestones are met. Once they are, the opportunity can be then moved to the Negotiating stage.
- o After the proposal has been delivered, the prospect has made additional contact to request some type of change, addition or reduction of product, pricing, terms, etc.
- o The prospect has conveyed that they are willing to commit within the current month if an agreement can be reached (also called a verbal commitment).

NEGOTIATING: Also referred to as your **30-day funnel**.
The prospect wants to change some element of your proposed solution.

The probability of closing an opportunity at this stage of the sales cycle is approximately 100%. While the probability is approximately 100%, you should have at least 150% more opportunities than you need to close in this stage of the funnel. The reason that the probability is 100% is because at this phase of the sales cycle, there are no more issues to resolve and the sale will absolutely, 100% close.

The only question is, will it close won or close lost? Because of this unknown, you want to have more opportunity than you really need in this stage. In an ideal world of negotiating, a verbal commitment to buy has been made by the prospect in this stage, and the details of the agreement are being worked out.

The opportunities in this stage should serve as your **"plan A deals,"** meaning that you should be forecasting these to close during the current month as long as the timeline and resources are aligned.

Involve others in this stage. The worst thing you can do is lose a deal, but the second-worst thing you can do is to lose alone. Your leadership and peer group should have experience or expertise that you lack in various situations or have ideas that could help you.

Milestones that must be met in order to place an opportunity in this stage:
o After the proposal has been delivered, the prospect has made additional contact to request some type of change, addition or reduction of product, pricing, terms, etc.
o The prospect has conveyed that they are willing to commit within the current month if an agreement can be reached.

The opportunity will stay in the Negotiate stage until the following milestones are met. Once they are, the opportunity can be moved to the Closed stage.
o The prospect has agreed to the terms and to move forward with you. Move the opportunity to **Closed Won**.
o The prospect tells you that they have decided to *not* move forward with your solution. Move the opportunity to **Closed Lost**. Follow the steps outlined in Closed Lost closely.

CLOSED WON/LOST:
You have either won or learned.

In this stage, you have either successfully won the sale, converting the prospect to a client, or your proposal has been rejected and you have lost the sale, but no doubt learned a lot about what to do or not to do so that you can win the sale in the future.

If you won: Congratulations—but now the hard work begins. Do what you told the prospect you would do with passion and conviction and follow step five of this process very closely to successfully serve the client.

If you lost: Do three things. First, do not react poorly, blowing any chance of doing business with the prospect in the future. Remember, it's not personal—it's business. You should handle a *no* as a *"not yet."*

Second, LEARN. Do your best to determine why you lost the sale and then work with your leadership or peers to determine if anything else could be done to win the deal.

If you can't win the deal after another attempt and the deal is truly lost, the third thing you must do is determine how soon you can follow up and create a robust follow-up plan. The reason for this is that I have lost many sales only to follow up a few weeks later to learn that the company the prospect selected had botched the delivery, installation or other elements of the deal. I converted losses to wins only a few days or weeks after losing it.

If that isn't the case, create a follow-up schedule to touch base with them in three months, six months and a few months prior to the expiration of the contract term they entered. You want to follow up prior to the contract term expiration in case you can get a jump on your competitor. Create this plan using your CRM, SFA or calendar tools so you can stay on track with all elements of your follow-up plan.

In sales, NO just means, "not now."

Step Three– Understanding Prospects and Clients– Recap

- Be intent on becoming an active listener as this is half of what it takes to understand prospects and clients.
- Be naturally curious about everything that has anything to do with your prospect.
- Be a problem seeker. If you can find and expose business problems, you can close sales by solving problems.
- Become an expert questioner. Ask what, who, when, where and why questions.
- Ask the prospect why they decided to take the meeting with you. Pay close attention to the answer because if you can solve this, you can more than likely earn the sale.
- Use a balance of open-ended and closed probes to get the prospect to open up about their business and business problems.
- Use the BART qualifying method to ensure you should continue investing in that prospect.

- Use the SIIR. question model to create a sense of urgency or to uncover a need that may be hidden.
- Use a sales funnel and keep it full and flowing. Put only real opportunities in it and classify them correctly and very accurately in the proper stage and ensure that they meet all of the milestones before progressing them along.
- Use the rule of 1/3s to better determine how many opportunities you need at any given stage.
- If you lose an opportunity, handle the loss with dignity and understand that *no* just means *not now*. Create a follow-up plan and win the opportunity at a later date.

"Start working with your prospects as if they've already hired you."

– Jill Konrath

Best Friends Forever

STEP 4: PARTNERING WITH PROSPECTS

"I'll be your best friend."

– Cameron (age 5)

Now that you fully understand the prospect, it's time to start partnering. In this step, you will learn the parallel between how kids and successful sales professionals clearly articulate the ways in which their product is perfect for the prospect through colorful storytelling, powerful presentations and shrewd negotiations.

In this step, your intent to help will be tested. You must remain true to your honest desire to help prospects. It will be very difficult to partner if your intent is merely to sell them something and move on. In many discussions at this point, where appropriate, in order to establish this sense of partnering, I will actually sit on the same side of the table as the prospect.

"I just know this will happen!"– Kids are perpetual optimists!

One of my favorite things about young children is the fact that they are naturally so optimistic and not only will they not take *no* for an answer, but they will FIND A WAY TO *YES*! Kids truly believe anything is possible and keep us adults on our toes and in check by asking, "Why not?"

My kids will sometimes ask if we can go get ice cream. When I tell them *no*, they immediately ask why not. When I tell them a "conditioned response" excuse like, "because it is too late," they immediately pull a list of places up on their smartphone and let me know that there are in fact places still open, and since I have money and a car, we could very easily make the trip. In fact, if you know a kid who is pessimistic, just understand that this is a learned behavior.

The most successful sales professionals I know are also some of the most optimistic people I know. In sales, you must have CONVICTION and BELIEVE that you work for the best company, selling the best products at the very best value out there. That belief and conviction are actually visible, believe it or not. People can *see* and *feel* them. People hate being sold, but most people love to buy and love buying from people with natural passion, belief and conviction. The partnership process starts with these ideals of conviction and finding a way to *yes*.

"Tell me the facts and I'll learn. Tell me the truth and I'll believe. But tell me a story and it will live in my heart forever."

– Native American proverb

"Once upon a time . . ."– Kids are the best storytellers!

My son once told me a riveting, 35-minute story that I would have sworn was real until about five minutes from the end, when he got to the part about fire-breathing dragons. Kids have a natural knack for storytelling and do it with such passion and descriptive details, painting vivid mental images and putting you inside of the story.

In sales, you must be able to tell your story—not about your product or service, but about how you and your product or service could benefit the prospect. A sale is an emotional transaction first, and the prospect must be able to not only believe logically, but feel emotionally, how you could benefit them and satisfy a want or need, or both. This is when the sale is actually made. The rest of the sales journey is just about the details of making the transaction work.

A sale is first closed in the prospect's mind, like a switch that goes on after they feel the product or service can satisfy what they need or want. Storytelling helps turn on that switch.

Part art and part science, storytelling is the best way to connect your solution to the prospect. The art part is being able to immerse yourself in whatever you are talking about with belief and conviction while taking the listeners on a journey. You must understand that they don't know your story, so filling in the details with as much *color* as possible by creating mental imagery and evoking emotion is critical.

The science part involves doing all of that in an interesting, concise and professional manner. You should map out your stories to ensure you capture all of these parts. It helps when you know your product's strengths and weaknesses, along with those of your competitors. While you can use marketing materials and visuals to assist, I recommend that you learn to tell stories without them, especially at first.

Keep in mind that storytelling can be used to discuss and explain things throughout the entire process. In my example, I will tell a story for the purpose of gaining the interest of an indifferent prospect. My goal is to get her interested enough to at least allow me to do a formal presentation about my product. I follow a map to organize my story.

An example of my story map:
For this example, I will be selling crop irrigation systems. (I have never sold irrigation systems and wanted to pick something I was unfamiliar with to show you how this map works when selling anything.)

What do I sell? Crop irrigation systems.

Who is my target prospect? Farmers, especially ones with aging irrigation systems or crop yield issues.

What did I learn about what is at stake as a result of my questioning about what happens if the current product doesn't function properly? (Cause of prospect anxiety): The tangible stakes are that the prospect could lose her crops and tens of thousands of dollars if the irrigation system fails by either delivering too much or too little water or failing to function altogether. The intangible stakes are that the farmer could lose hundreds of hours of hard work, suffer damage to her professional reputation and become very frustrated if the system fails.

What does the best-case scenario look like for the prospect? The best case is the famer's crops are ready for harvest ahead of schedule and are bigger and healthier than anticipated.

Why is my product better than (or what sets it apart from) those of my competitors? Mine is:
- Manufactured from heavy-gauge materials that last nearly twice as long as my competitor's.
- Digitally controlled with sensors that modify water distribution for optimal hydration for *specific crops.*
- Significantly more expensive than my competitor's.

Mental imagery I should use:
- Anxiety image: Fields of over- or under-watered crops. Past-due bank notes. Hard work that doesn't pay off.
- Best-case scenario image: Fields of healthy, oversized crops, ready for harvest ahead of schedule. Someone or something working on her behalf.

My story to Farmer Annie

Annie, thanks for taking the time to answer all of my questions and for sharing your insights on the importance of crop irrigation. When I think of the hours and hours of hard work, early mornings and long days you put into this farm, the thought of waking up one morning and gazing out on an entire field of wasted, over- or under-watered crops gives me anxiety—and I'm not even a farmer!

Imagine, if you will, a virtual farmer, out here helping share some of the burden and hard work of crop irrigation. What if you had someone or something that, like you, knows what types of crops were planted and could actively monitor the soil conditions, and worked even while you slept?

Based on the soil conditions and types of crops, desired yield weight and time to harvest, this virtual farmer automatically adjusts hydration perfectly to not only sustain the crops, but to increase both weight of the crop, while also speeding up the time to harvest.

Now, imagine waking up to the perfect sunrise shining brightly on your fields of full, healthy and ready-to-harvest crops that will satisfy the bank notes and then some!

This product not only exists, but lasts twice as long as anything like it on the market. And while it can be a significant investment for such a solution, because of larger crop sizes and faster times to harvest, this solution pays for itself in only one or two seasons. I'd like the opportunity to present my product formally and give you the chance to see what it has been able to do for other farmers in your situation.

Now, that may not be a perfect story and may even have a few inaccurate statements due to my inexperience with the farming industry, but let me call out what I was able to do. I used descriptive words that painted mental images like *waking up one morning and gazing out on an entire field of wasted, over- or under-watered crops.* I knew how much she values hard work, so I was careful to refer to my product as additional help that knew things only she did, and that worked even while she slept.

I also continued to reinforce what my product did for her and gave her a mental image of an ideal scenario of fields full of healthy crops. The statistics and features are irrelevant if I can't tie them back to what is important to her. Create similar maps and tell powerful stories that help prospects envision and imagine what your product can do for them!

"Now that's funny!"– Kids love (and use) humor!

I invited a few work colleagues to my home one night to discuss some major changes that were about to take place. I also shared the anxiety I was feeling with my son, who was ten years old at the time.

He asked why I was so nervous, and I told him that it was a tense situation, but that everything would be fine. He assured me that everything would be fine and told me I should share a joke to put everyone at ease. I told him I didn't feel as if the situation warranted a joke, but thanked him anyway.

That evening, my son interrupted my discussion with the group as soon as he noticed the tension mounting.

He said in a loud voice and with a puzzled face, "Dad, I need to ask you something! Have you heard of that new movie called "Constipation?"
Me (with an even more puzzled face): "No."
Son (grinning ear to ear): "I guess it hasn't come out yet!"

Come on, you didn't think you would get through an entire book on kid tactics without reading a poop joke, did you?

"Like a welcome summer rain, humor may suddenly cleanse and cool the earth, the air and you." –Langston Hughes

---

The bottom line is the group laughed hysterically and it eased an otherwise very tense situation. My son knew that interjecting humor could ease a tense situation and this is perhaps the only time I've been glad he didn't take my direction.

While I am not advising you to tell poop jokes to your work colleagues , I do believe that introducing humor to tense situations (or situations that tend to become tense) can ease the tension if done appropriately.

Look for these opportunities to add humor because at the end of the day, people buy from people *and* scientifically speaking, people are the only animals in the world that have the capacity for humor and laughter. Other animals can mimic a laugh but do not process humor.

"What if we did this?" – Kids will make a proposal you can't refuse!

Kids always have some proposal for what to do or what could be done, and I love the innocence of believing that anything is possible. "What if?" is one of the most powerful and most underutilized questions in a sales professional's arsenal. At worst, asking *what if* gets people to think about what they are (or are not) willing to do, and *you can build on that*.

It doesn't make a lot of sense to go into great detail about building proposals here, because quotes, how to build them, and what to include in each proposal varies by company and industry.

There are, however, a few things that your proposal delivery should include:

1. Do your best to deliver your proposal in person and never over the phone or email, unless your proximity or the prospect simply won't permit it. By delivering the proposal in person, you are able to read body language and ask questions that are applicable to that body language.

2. Find a way to include your ability to positively impact the intangibles, such as reduced frustration, improved reputation, etc.

3. Simplify your proposal so that the message of how you can meet the prospect's expectations doesn't get lost in a bottom-line number. If your proposal involves different options, don't give too many as this may only confuse the prospect and delay your sale.

4. Recap all of the benefits your product will provide and tie them directly to the prospect's needs and wants.

5. Don't just hand the proposal to the prospect—present it!

"Now presenting . . . me!" Kids are very proud presenters!

Every year when my kids were in elementary school, the school held what they called a "wax museum," where the kids were all tasked with learning several key facts about a famous person in history, dress like them and stand perfectly still in the hall, like a wax figure. When parents walked up and pressed a makeshift button on the wall next to the child, the child would animate to present the facts they learned.

The kids really got into it. They would insist on getting the correct wig, make up or attire that accurately matched their character. When that button was pressed, they came alive, beaming with pride as they spouted off fact after fact about "their" life and how interesting they were. I loved that it gave young kids an opportunity to prepare and present something they were passionate about. I was always impressed with how great they were, despite (or perhaps because) they *didn't* have any type of formal presentation training. It also solidified my belief that kids are naturally great presenters.

How important are presentation skills to us as sales professionals? Most professional sales organizations rank the ability to present well as one of the skills they look for most when recruiting.

Most people think of a presentation as a grand stage with PowerPoint slides in front of a large audience. This usually is not the case at all. In sales, you are presenting constantly.

In fact, you make a series of small presentations within each step of the sales process. When you are prospecting and attempting to get prospects to accept a meeting with you, you present the benefits of such a meeting.

When you open a sales call, you present why the prospect should listen to you. When you get to the Understand step, you present information on why the client should answer your questions. And now, in the stage of Partnering, you must present why the prospect should decide to buy your product over all the others.

When giving any presentation, it is important to keep what is important to the prospect in mind at all times. In fact, you should center the presentation around them and how your product would benefit them.

Before you begin a presentation, it is important that you first re-establish rapport and ask the prospect if anything has changed since you last met. This way, you can adjust your message on the fly in case something like the decision-making process or any needs have changed.

Before you even start preparing, you must understand that the presentation is YOU (not a slide deck) and ABOUT THEM (how your product connects to their needs and wants). A presentation is not about the dazzling visual aids—it's all about what you say.

In some cases, slides and other visual aids are appropriate, in which case you should be very selective with what you include. Less is more with visuals, especially slides. Even with highly technical products, you should strive to have as few slides as possible. Each one must be absolutely critical. Do not include anything that would make you say to the prospect, "We can skip over this." If you don't need to talk about it, do not include it, period. Again, less is more.

It is not what you communicate, but what gets communicated.

I created the checklist to help me get my points and priorities together every time I present. I ask myself a series of "did I?" questions.

DID I:

- ⊘ **Invite the right people to the presentation based on what I learned from my BART questions?**
  Go back through your BART questions, making sure you have done everything you can to get all of the decision makers in the room to hear your presentation. Those who are enthusiastic enough to buy aren't always enthusiastic or educated enough to sell to those not present, so do your best to get all decision makers in the room when you present.

- ⊘ **Build a review of, and prioritize, the client's needs and wants, along with their impacts (tangible and intangible) to the prospect?**
  I always recap what I learned from the prospect about their business problems and the specific impact these problems have on their business, along with the people affected.

- ⊘ **Build a general overview of my solution and specific talking points about its direct benefits?**
  What matters is not what my product does—it is what my product does FOR THEM. I need to carefully tie both the prospect's needs and wants to how my product can satisfy those needs and wants. Be careful to focus on both, as many prospects will be driven by what they want more than what they need. After all, most people don't *need* leather seats in a car, they *want* them! Not that there aren't certain benefits to leather seats, such as being stain resistant, etc., but most people will come up with ways to justify them as a need. All industries have a "leather seat" option available.

⊘ **Create my talking points in layman's terms?**
I often hear the mistake of salespeople using terms known only to their industry or even to their specific company. Using industry-specific jargon in the industry the prospect works in is okay, but keep in mind that if you have a CFO in the room, he or she may not understand the terms and if they don't, the presentation is no longer about THEM. You are failing and may not even realize it.

⊘ **Build in simple-to-understand technical specifications and requirements?**
Regardless of how complex your solution is, there is a way to describe it in terms that make it simple for the prospect to understand. If your prospect has specifically asked for an explanation of any technical elements, then proceed, but be sure you tie in the concepts for everyone present. My preference is to have that presentation first so that I have technical buy in or the "yes, this product CAN work for you" discussion before I get to this point of selling the total solution.

⊘ **Prepare to involve the prospect in the presentation?**
A formal presentation should very much include the prospect. You can do this by asking questions along the way, like, "How do you see this working for you?" or, "Would this color work for you, or is a different color better?" Use any question that gets the prospect to buy in and become engaged in what you are saying. You also want the prospect agreeing with you or agreeing to as many topics as you can throughout the presentation, even if it just on the color, style or product configuration.

⊘ **Summarize how the prospect's needs link directly to how my product or service meets those needs?**
This is critical to ensuring that the prospect understands how my product will solve their specific business problems. I do this by creating a side-by-side list of the prospect's problems and how my product will solve them.

⊘ **Build a return on investment (ROI) that showcases the value as
cost—and not just the price—of my solution simply and
effectively, using information I gathered in my SIIR.
questioning model?**

Now is the time to use what you learned about the problem's
serious impact on the prospect's business and turn it into an ROI
model to justify the price of your solution. This is especially the
case when the prospect doesn't currently have in place what you
are offering. They will need to justify something without being
able to compare it to what is currently in place and need an ROI
model.

This is important because the *price* of your product may be
considered high, but when broken down in an ROI model, the *cost*
maybe extremely low. Or, the product might pay for itself in a
short time through the benefits it provides. ROIs can be very
effective and fairly easy to build if you have asked the right
questions in the SIIR. process.

To build a quick ROI, take the tangible, hard cost of what the
problem costs the prospect in dollars and multiply that times how
many times it happens, and then by how many people it happens
to in order to get a total. Do this for each of the business problems
you uncovered. That total is usually so substantial that it
outweighs the cost of your solution. Even if it doesn't, it will
offset the cost so greatly that the prospect is usually willing to
entertain implementing your solution when they see its value
compared to their current business model.

If I sold cameras for automated car washes, for example, my ROI model
might look like this:

Example ROI for "Carl's Car Wash"
Total cost of my camera solution for all three locations: $50,000
Carl's Car Wash's business problem: Customers claim car damage that
the car wash did not cause, but since they have no way of proving it, they
are liable.

Carl's hard cost to repair one car when an owner claims it was damaged in the washing process: $3,000
Multiplied by the number of claims each year: 9
Multiplied by the number of car wash locations: in Carl's case, 3
Grand total of hard costs annually because of this problem: $81,000

ROI Summary: Based on the bottom-line math, my solution would pay for itself in a little over eight months and then begin saving the prospect as much as $81,000 annually. This is what I present to the prospect in a very clear and simple format.

In some cases, hard costs alone will not compel the prospect to take action. When that is the case, I focus on the intangible factors I learned in my discovery by focusing on things like how the problem frustrated the prospect or wasted a great deal of time. These intangibles still impact the prospect's overall **Finance**, **Image** or **Productivity** in one way or another.

Carl's additional concerns: False claims damaged the company's image. Sales declined (Finance) each time a false claim was disputed because of the backlash on social media. The car wash suffered damage to the brand, hurting potential market expansion (Finance). While this is not impossible to quantify, it can be difficult. The prospect will understand this as an added cost they are incurring, one that your product could help eliminate.

The prospect's other concern, which I uncovered, is the time it takes to deal with all of the false claims (Productivity). It takes hours each month to process each claim and decide if it is worth fighting. This is time taken away from the prospect's ability to grow, market and expand the car wash (Finance and Productivity). While this involves the tangible cost of hourly wages, the prospect was more upset about the frustration it caused than the money spent, so I highlight how my product can almost entirely eliminate frustration, as well.

⊘ **Can you outline a catalyst (such as an upcoming deadline) to establish a timeline so we can move toward a close?**
Using an event such as an upcoming meeting, fiscal year end or other deadline is helpful in progressing deals along. I will have either identified this deadline or tried to create one, such as promoting the idea of the prospect having a staff or safety meeting so that we can use that date as the implementation date and work backward from there. When I present, I use that as the drop-dead date and work backwards in my timeline to get the prospect's buy in on any additional steps that need to happen before then, such as signing an agreement, placing an order, choosing options, and so on.

⊘ **Gain commitment along the way?**
As mentioned in a previous checkpoint, you want to get agreement throughout the presentation. To do this, build in a series of small checkpoints where you can ask for agreement. Start with simple, obvious ones and build up to harder ones like dates or agreement on terms and conditions.

⊘ **Practice "what ifs"?**
Any time you are about to present or attend a sales call, you should practice "what ifs." These are simply a series of questions that identify anything that might happen on the call that you couldn't handle. Here are several common ones, but you should build your own that are more specific to your company, industry and company:
- What if the prospect only gives me ten minutes instead of the hour we agreed on?
- What if my laptop crashes?
- What if the power goes out during my presentation?
- What if all of the people who committed to being there aren't there?
- What if more people than committed to being there show up?
- What if I spill coffee on my suit on my way there?

"Are we there yet?" – Kids are natural closers!

Children are usually very conscious of where they are in a process, such as a road trip, and will frequently ask the dreaded question, "Dad, are we there yet?" If I had a dollar for every time I heard "Are we there yet?" I would have retired years ago. While most parents know first-hand that this question can be annoying, it is an important question for a child to ask in order to find out where they are in the process.

The partner process steps can be intense, so let's recap so you know precisely where you are and how to continue to move to the close.

Right now, based on the five steps, you are at the stage where you have achieved the following: successfully (1) **uncovered** a good prospect that has the propensity to buy from you. You enthusiastically (2) **opened** the sales call with value, purpose and structure, understanding that the prospect is interested in how you can positively impact their FIP (Finance,

Image and/or Productivity). You then probed with strategic questions to truly (3) **understand** what the prospect wants, along with the what, when, who, how, where and why of the prospect's business problems. You have carefully captured how these needs and wants are prioritized and recorded them accurately in your funnel.

Now ready to (4) **partner**, you have told rich, colorful stories that use powerful imagery to highlight how your product would complement their business, moving them to see themselves using your product. You have at last built a proposal and a formal presentation and successfully presented your proposal, technical specifications and ability to meet prospect requirements, along with pricing, and overall cost with a compelling ROI, all in a deeply meaningful manner.

But . . . "are we there yet?" At this point, can we go ahead and close with confidence?

The fastest and most direct way to close is to ask a direct closing question such as, "It seems like we can solve your problems, so what do you think?" Or, "Can I earn your business today?" Or, "What do you say we proceed?" While these are simple phrases, many salespeople don't want to utter them. The best reason I can guess is because if the prospect says no, they feel as if they have lost. Again, I go back to the rule I shared with you earlier: You want to close fast or lose fast.

You can move the sale along by asking a closing question—if you ask it at the appropriate time. It will either move the sale to the "closed won" status or let you know what gap you must still overcome to close the sale.

But when is the appropriate time? When you can answer *yes* to the following:

- ✓ Can you solve the prospect's problems?
- ✓ Will it make business sense for them to buy your product?
- ✓ Have you effectively qualified the prospect to ensure they have the available resources and proper people committed to this project?
- ✓ Is the timeline clearly established?
- ✓ Can you clearly articulate how you, your company and product can solve the prospect's business problems in a positive way?
- ✓ Do they care? Have you instilled some level of urgency? (If not, go back to the SIIR. questions and probe for additional business problems.)

Then the time is appropriate to ask a direct closing question.

It will be hard to progress the sale if you don't ask for it.

Another way to successfully finalize a deal, as mentioned earlier, is to use an important date, such as an upcoming meeting or significant event, as a catalyst. If there is no significant date approaching, use the start of a new year, month or quarter as a theoretical deadline and work backwards from that.

To do this, I show the prospect a printed calendar and ask what date makes the most sense for them to actually get the product in hand. I then discuss the time it takes to get their account established, the order placed, the shipping time, and other variables. This establishes the last day when they could decide to go forward with my solution and still meet their deadline. And yes (in my experience, anyway), I have found that even if the deadline is completely made up, people will still work to meet it.

MONTH March						
Sunday	Monday	Tuesday	Wednesday	Thursday	Friday	Saturday
25	26	27	28	29	30	31
	Sign Agreement	Create Client Account	Place order	Shipping	Proposed Rollout Date	

The other way I have found to cross the bridge of successfully closing a deal is by asking the prospect if they have answered the "should I" questions. The theory here is that we all need answers on three fundamental questions before we feel good about investing in anything significant.

You may not have seen these questions before, but I promise that you have asked them of yourself before making a major purchase. I will give you the primary three questions and some commentary that provides more clarity on specifically what they might be thinking regarding that question. After I outline the questions, I will walk you through an example and explain how to position these questions to the prospect.

Here are the "should I" questions:

1. **Should I change?** Why would we (the prospect) choose to change?
   - Is the pain of doing nothing greater than the pain of changing?
   - Does changing make business sense?
   - Does this change add value? If so, is it short-term or long-term value?
   - Does the change offer any intangible benefits such as making my job easier, improving client retention, etc.?
   - Does this change help us meet our higher-level goals/objectives?

2. **Should I choose this particular solution?** Why would we (the prospect) choose *your* solution for this project?
   - Will it work?
   - Is there an ROI?
   - Are the benefits of this solution greater than those of competitors?
   - Is the company offering the solution one I would do business with?
   - Is the representative offering the solution someone I would do business with?
   - Are all of the decision makers in my organization willing to sign off on this solution?

3. **Should I do this now?** Why would we (the prospect) move forward with this project now?
   - Will changing now help us in terms of saving time or money, making my job easier, making the situation better for our clients, etc.?
   - Is there a scarcity of product?
   - Is there financial motivation, such as pricing or promotions?
   - Is not changing costing more each day than this solution would cost to implement?
   - Is there a competitive advantage to making this change sooner rather than later?
   - Is there a deadline that must be met?

If you think about something as simple as purchasing a vehicle, for example, these questions apply.

Here is how.

Consider some need or want that comes up. For example, you get a job and need transportation, you need a larger car to accommodate a new baby or perhaps you just want something sporty to show off.

You will ask yourself the "should I change?" question when you look at purchasing a vehicle. Whether it's "Why change the car I have now?" or "Why change and purchase a car at all?" you ask yourself the question the "should I change" question subconsciously.

Next, you ask yourself, "Should I choose this specific car?" Do you need something economical in order to inexpensively commute long distances? Or a large truck so you can haul things or tow trailers or other vehicles? In any case, you ask yourself the "why this solution?" question. Many things come into play with this question, as here is where the prospect will also ask themselves about you—the salesperson—and mentally evaluate both the company and the individual selling the product they are considering.

And finally, the question becomes, "Should I do this now?" Could the purchase wait, or is there a date looming (such as the birth of a child) that means your sporty two-seater is no longer the best choice? Or are you moving or changing jobs, relationships, or another major life situation? As is the case with the other questions, you will ask, "Why now?" even if just subconsciously.

Just knowing there are "three *why* questions" gives you a strategic sales advantage that you may not have had before because you know the prospect will need these questions satisfied even if they don't know to ask these questions.

In fact, the reason many deals stall is because the prospect hasn't gotten the answers to one or more of the "should I" questions and may not even know to articulate them.

That said, it is important that you use the knowledge you have gained appropriately and help guide the prospect to the best answers to these questions. In situations when it felt right, I have written these three questions down on paper and placed them in front of the prospect.

I then asked, "Do you feel like you have answers to these questions? Because I have learned that it is my job to ensure you have the answers to these very important questions before you will feel comfortable enough to move forward with changing, specifically to my solution."

I mean, why not? What do I have to lose, if I have done all of the other parts correctly? I want to truly partner with the prospect, and this is a great way to show them that I don't just want them to change, I want them fully satisfied with their decision to change.

"No? But why not?"– Kids can handle objections!

Anytime you tell a kid *no*, you expect them to ask, "But, why not?" It is a built-in response we have as kids and it is not asked to understand and accept the answer. Instead, we ask in order to understand the objection and overcome the initial negative response!

We are conditioned from an early age to not accept—or to at least question—when we are told *no*. Not much changes as we age and that is especially the case for those of us in sales, since being told *no* typically means we are not going to be paid. But simply asking "Why not?" isn't enough when it comes to handling and overcoming objections. In some cases, you will need to negotiate (a topic we will discuss later), but in some cases, you may simply need to offer proof or clarify something in order to close the deal. Here is how to deal with being told *no*.

Great news! Objections mean the sale is still alive!

First, it is important that you **never interrupt, react or even respond immediately**, but remain calm and pause for a few seconds before responding. You don't want to be seen as defensive—that is not what partners do. You are on their side, after all. Next, you will want to **listen to the entire objection**. Sometimes, as soon as we are told *no*, we almost mentally shut down and stop hearing anything else. It is important to actively listen to the entire objection.

A great way to ensure you are aligned with how the prospect is thinking and feeling is to **restate the objection to make sure you fully understand** what is being disputed. An example: "If I understand you correctly, you don't wish to move forward with the proposed solution because you don't believe it is as reliable as our competitor's—is that correct?"

After you fully understand the objection, go ahead and **(but don't agree with)** the objection. When you are being told *no* and given a reason such as, they believe your competitor is better than you, you can affirm that you understand, just don't agree and say something like, "Okay, fantastic!" or "I agree with you." This response reinforces the prospect's belief that they may not need your product. It's ironic, but many salespeople will quickly agree with the prospect out of shock or in an attempt to align with the prospect, not realizing that it only solidifies the prospect's decision to go a different route. Instead, say phrases like, "I see," "I understand," or "Okay." There is a big difference physiologically between affirming and agreeing.

Ask clarifying questions until you fully understand the objection. Let the naturally curious and inquisitive kid in you come out. Ask questions like, "May I ask why?" or, "Can you tell me more about that?" or, "What information did you use to determine that?" Again, you must follow these steps, or these questions can be perceived as very defensive. A prospect who tells a salesperson *no* is already in a defensive state and this is another reason why sales stall.

The bottom line is that few prospects want to be the bearer of bad news. Many times, the prospect has thoroughly worked out and justified the decision, so asking these questions will move them from this otherwise rehearsed response and allow you to understand the real reasoning behind their decision. You should **write down the concerns as you uncover them** and dig in to discover the who, what, when, where and why as you may be able to use that information in your rebuttal. You want to be sure that you probe to find out if they have any other concerns so you can be prepared to handle them all. Finally, after resolving an objection, **confirm** with the prospect that the concern is resolved.

At this point, you will want to **affirm again and again**, after each exchange, letting the prospect know that you both hear *and* understand each objection as they have stated it.

The conversation might sound like this:
Prospect: "I'm sorry, but we are going with your competitor."
Me (Affirm): "I see." (Clarify): "May I ask why?"
Prospect: "It came down to price and they are 20% cheaper than you guys."
Me (Affirm again): "I understand." (Clarify): "Are they offering you a similar product and the same terms as we are?"
Prospect: "Almost. The product is slightly smaller than yours and their terms are spread out just one year longer than yours, but it should work for what we need."

Me (Affirm again): "Okay. I see."
Me: (Ask about other concerns): "Was the 20% lower price the only concern that kept you from moving forward with us?
Prospect: "Yes."

If the prospect had said *no* to the last question, indicating that they had **multiple concerns**, you would want to **write down the first concern and then repeat the process for all concerns, addressing each one separately**.

Next, you want to **make a smooth transition** before moving to resolve the objection. Transitions are critical because they help the prospect prepare to see things from a different perspective or to re-examine something they might have missed. You can take the onus here for potentially missing something, so the prospect doesn't feel as if they are wrong for feeling the way they do, or for making the decision they made.

Transitions can immediately follow an affirmation and can be as subtle as a quick exchange like this:

Me (Affirm): "I see." (Transition) "Would you mind if we looked at the two choices side by side? I may have a few ideas that would work."

Prospect: "Well, we have already made our decision, so no thanks."

Me (PERSIST): "I totally understand, but I just wouldn't feel right if I missed something that could have helped you." (onus)

Prospect: "Okay. I suppose we could take a quick look at it."

Now you must **determine what type of objection you have received**. Prospects pose several types of objections and a different resolution method is used for each.

"Knowledge has to be improved, challenged, and increased constantly, or it vanishes." - Peter Drucker

---

The first type of objection we will look at is misunderstanding or confusion.

Misunderstanding: Misunderstandings happen when there is *confusion* about something the prospect has heard, seen or believes to be a fact. Misunderstanding unravels sales quickly and must be handled delicately so that the prospect doesn't feel stupid or that they have missed something simple they should have understood.

If you have any foolish pride or ego in you, now is the time to get rid of it. I have seen misunderstandings handled so poorly, that one of two things happen. Either the prospect not only stays with their original decision not to do business with the salesperson (if for no other reason than to spite them), or the interaction sours any future dealings because the prospect has been made to feel stupid.

Transitions toward resolving a misunderstanding are more critical than the actual review of information to gain clarity. You want to follow the same steps outlined here when handling an objection, and listen, affirm, restate for clarity, affirm again and ask about any other concerns before transitioning and responding. The difference is that you have more ownership or "onus" of the situation and zero ego involvement, and you always end by confirming that you have successfully addressed their objections.

An exchange where there is a misunderstanding may sound like this:

Prospect: "We're sorry, but we are going with your competitor."

Me (Affirm): "I see."

Me (Clarify): "May I ask why?"

Prospect: "It came down to price and they are 20% cheaper than you guys."

Me (Affirm again): "I understand." (Clarify) "Are they offering you a similar product and under the same terms as we are?"

Prospect: "Almost. The product is slightly smaller than yours and their terms are spread out just one year longer than yours, but it should work for what we need."

Me (Affirm again): "Okay. I see." (Ask about other concerns): "Was the 20% lower price the only concern that kept you from moving forward with us?"

Prospect: "Yes."

Me (Affirm): "Okay." (Transition with ownness): "I feel terrible! I am not sure I included our similar configuration on page two of the proposal. Would you mind if we take a quick look at it? I wouldn't want my mistake to deter you from making the best decision for the business." (onus of not including it in the proposal even though I did and asking if we can take another look.)

Prospect: "Sure. Maybe I just missed it."

Me (Full ownness): "I'm sure it was me either not including it or not covering it well enough. In either case, let's review it because the great news is that we offer that configuration, as well."

Prospect: "There it is, right there! So sorry I missed that."

Me (Confirming): "No worries at all! Does that answer the concern?"

Another type of objection is when a prospect is skeptical.

Skeptical: When a prospect is skeptical, they are simply expressing doubt. They *doubt* something they have seen, heard or perceive to be a fact. While this maybe the simplest objection to overcome if handled properly, it can and will cause a sale to be lost as quickly as any objection.

The way you remove doubt is with proof. But what kind of proof? The answer: whatever kind of proof the prospect wants. I have seen this objection not be overcome because the wrong type of proof was offered. For example, if the prospect doubts your product can function in a certain way, you won't convince them by showing them a full color, marketing slick that says otherwise. The key here is to *ask the prospect* what they would like to see that would clear up the doubt.

But first, **transition**.

Me (Transition): "I can appreciate you being skeptical, and I know it does seem like it can do a lot." (Ask about proof): "What proof would you like to see that would make you feel better about the products' functionality?"

Even though a product demonstration in the prospect's own environment will usually quash any doubt, you should always ask. I also have seen cases where prospects ask for a client testimonial or another burden of proof. What counts is satisfying what they want to see. And as is the case with a misunderstanding, after moving to resolve, you must be sure to confirm that you have successfully answered their objection.

"Extraordinary claims require extraordinary evidence."

—Carl Sagan

The final type of objection we will cover is the conditional objection.

Conditional: Conditional objections occur when you, your company or product fail to meet one or more of the needs, wants, specifications or *conditions* the prospect expressed. It could also be that a competitor or the current situation is seen as better. Alternatively, there could be something behind the stated condition that you didn't uncover in the Understanding step of the process that is leading to them to decline the offer.

A good example in my experience has been when the prospect disputes the price, when in fact they have had budget cuts and bigger sales revenue problems that they are trying to solve. In this case, lowering the price of my product is only a surface-level need in front of a much larger need. And yes, this can happen even if the prospect finds value in your offer.

For you as the sales professional, it goes back to gathering as much information as you can so you can potentially explain how paying slightly more for your product could add value by helping them grow revenue or cut costs in another part of the business. Doing this helps overcome the real concern, which is revenue. This is why staying focused on *business* problems and not merely specific product problems is so important in the Understand step of this process. Occasionally there is no underlying need behind a conditional objection, and it is simply that your product can't do a certain thing or is priced higher than what the prospect is willing to pay.

If you get a conditional objection, ***and*** *you still believe that your product is the best choice for the prospect,* the first step is to STOP and do the following: Follow the same rules for handling any objection and *listen* to the entire objection without interruption, *affirm* and then carefully go back through the *question* model and do your best to fully understand the condition and anything behind the condition that may help you build a compelling case for your product to still be the best choice.

Next, encourage the prospect to pause and look at things objectively because while it might not meet one or more of the conditions, it might still be the best overall option. If you can't get the prospect to refocus on the overall scope of the business and how your product will play a positive role given these explanations, you might need to deploy one of the following negotiation tactics.

"I will clean my room if you let me have a sleepover!" - Kids are shrewd negotiators!

My kids, like most children, are not the best at sharing—especially my two boys. My older son's all-time favorite toy was a bright red wagon that he used for pulling around the neighborhood kids. His second-favorite toy of all time was a BMX bike that he loved riding through the dirt. While my younger son also had plenty of toys, both boys usually wanted only what the other had. On occasion my younger son would ask his brother if he could play with one of his toys, only to be quickly be told *no*!

That all changed one warm, summer day when my boys, seven and nine, were playing outside. I was cleaning out the garage and had everything from bikes to water balloons pulled out for them. Who played with what was different on this day because of my younger son's ability to negotiate.

My older son was pulling kids in his wagon when his brother approached and asked if he could use (of all things) his prized, red wagon.

"No way!" was the response.

Unphased, my younger son quickly followed up with, "Since I can't use the wagon, can I at least ride your bike?"

After a moment or two, my older son agreed, and for the first time ever, allowed his kid brother to ride his bike.

Just then, my younger son's friends all pulled up on their bikes and asked if he could go riding, to which he replied, "Yes, I can!" with a devilish grin.

My son never wanted his brother's wagon, but mastered a negotiation tactic that some sales professionals still haven't figured out: always ask for more than what you really want.

Aside from this skill, kids are effective negotiators because they do the following:

- **They pay attention to everything**. Kids notice the smallest, seemingly insignificant details—and these details can be used when it comes to pointing out certain things (good or bad) to people.

- **They don't give away more than they need to**. Usually, even when a kid can't use or finish what they have, they are still not willing to give up more than what they absolutely have to.

- **They know what people want**. My kids always knew they could at least get my attention with a cold Coca-Cola and that I was a sucker for a huge bear hug! Once we as sales professionals realize that all businesses want and care about *Finance, Image* and *Productivity* (FIP) and can stay focused on those issues, we can more effectively negotiate.

Kids use a variety of tactics to negotiate and close the sale, and so should you. When it comes to sales and overcoming conditional objections, you may have to deploy any number of the following negotiation tactics. In some cases, you may have to deploy more than one.

<u>Tactic 1.</u> – **Ask for more than what you want.** As noted in my son's bike story, asking for more than what you want can be effective in going after what you are really targeting to begin with. Remember that you can always go down, but it is very hard to go up, especially in price. Always start off by asking for more than what you want. (By the way, the prospect also knows this and will ask for more than they intend to get.)

This tactic works more often when you are concerned that the prospect will dispute your price. You might decide to quote the product with the most options so you can remove them and come down to your original price goal. I have seen this tactic used effectively in multiple industries.

<u>Tactic 2.</u> – **If you give, then get.** Never give up anything without getting something in return. I have watched many salespeople give concession after concession and get nothing in return. The prospect will ask for additional options, increased quantity or faster delivery and the salesperson will concede and get nothing in return. You may be thinking, what should they have gotten—isn't the sale enough? The short answer is *no*! If you give, you should get.

Here are some things you could ask for:
- TIME: Get the prospect to commit to the sale that day (or in some way sooner than anticipated).
- TERMS: Ask the prospect to agree to a longer commitment or different configuration of the terms.
- QUANTITY: Ask the prospect to buy more of what they are buying.
- QUALITY: Ask the prospect to buy a better version of what they are buying.
- REFERRALS: When appropriate, ask the prospect to bring along others who will also purchase if the concessions are met.
- ENDORSEMENT: Ask the prospect to publicly endorse your product or company as compensation in exchange for the requested concessions. *Just make sure this is legal and adheres to the policies of your industry and company.*

This tactic works more often when you get a request to change your proposal to provide more product or lower the cost.

<u>Tactic 3.</u> – **Reduce your offer.** This one makes a lot of salespeople uncomfortable, but sometimes sales is uncomfortable. When a prospect disputes something in your proposal—especially price—you can simply ask what aspect of the offer you should reduce in order to be able to meet that price. Think of it like this: if I sell grapes and the prospect wants to buy three pounds but has only enough money for two pounds, I would simply take away a pound, and no one would bat an eye. But if I sell cars and the price of the proposed, well-equipped car is $35,000, but the prospect only wants to pay $32,000, the first thing I would ask is how attached the prospect is to the leather seats. Because the great news is, we could meet that price by simply removing $3,000 worth of options.

This tactic works more often when a price is being disputed; you counter by offering to reduce the offer in some way that meets the requested price. This varies by product, company and industry, but you could choose to reduce the amount of time the prospect has access to the product, the amount of the product or the options included in the original proposal.

Tactic 4. – **Use an ROI model to establish more value.** Whenever price is questioned, move to providing an ROI model to negate the price of the product, even if one was presented originally. Showing a prospect a return on investment can be very effective if you are careful to use the numbers you gathered while in the Understanding step of the process. Go over the numbers again and ask if anything has changed and if the figures are accurate. Depending on the timeframe in which your product will provide a return on investment, ask them what they feel is a good ROI and then show them how you can meet or beat that with your product. If there is no ROI, one of two things is probably the case: your product is a luxury item, where ROI is hard to calculate because the product is more want than need, or it simply doesn't make good business sense for the prospect to buy your product at this time.

If there is no ROI, you should always do the right thing and let the prospect know that and set yourself up for another deal later on. I can still recall running every number I could find for a prospect and no matter how I sliced it, based on their circumstances, needs and even their wants, there was no good ROI for them. I let the prospect know that I had done some research on their behalf and while I didn't in good faith believe that it was a smart business decision for them to buy from me that day, my research uncovered some cost saving they could put into effect to save money on their current system. Almost one year later, the prospect's business went through some changes and I closed one of the largest sales of my careers. ROI or not, always do the right thing.

If you still believe your offer has overall value, despite it not having a positive or quick ROI, you may need to move on to the more applicable tactic, listed next.

Tactic 4 is best used when your product could benefit the prospect's overall business or larger priorities. You can show how an investment in your product now could be a good business decision at some point down the road. Keep in mind that different products and industries have different expectations of ROI.

Just because a six-month ROI isn't good in one industry doesn't mean that a six-year ROI isn't great in a different one.

<u>**Tactic 5.**</u> – **Break it down to the ridiculous.** When your proposal is higher than your competitor's, remember that you only have to sell the *difference*. In other words, if your proposal is for $10,000, and the competitor's offer is only $8,000, stop selling the $10,000 price tag and start selling the difference of $2,000. The prospect is essentially telling you that they have agreed to $8,000. A tactic I have used very successfully is to break the difference down to an annual, monthly, daily and then hourly cost difference. Once I amortize that amount across all the end users (if applicable) the difference is ridiculously small.

Here is an example of using this tactic in selling industrial work uniforms.

My proposal is for $10,000 for 100 new uniforms. My competitor's proposal for a similar, yet inferior, uniform is $8,000. When my prospect comes back and explains that they understand how my product is better, but also $2,000 higher than the alternative, I thank the prospect for the information and ask if we could look at the larger scope of the project as it relates to the cost of the uniforms.

If we just compare both uniforms as if they will last for one year of use, and divide the $2,000 price difference over the course of that year, the difference is $166.67.

$2,000 price difference / 12 months = $166.67 price difference.

If we divide that difference further by the week, the difference is $41.66 higher.

$166.67 / 4 weeks = $41.66 price difference.

If we look even deeper at the five days your workers wear the uniform each week, the cost difference is only $8.33 per day higher.
$41.66 / 5 days = $8.33 per day price difference.

But, if we look even closer at the price for the eight hours each day the worker wears the uniform, the price difference is only $1.04 per hour difference.
$8.33 / 8 hours = $1.04 per hour price difference.

When we divide the $1.04 cost per hour price difference over the 100 workers, **the cost difference of my product over my competitor's is literally one penny per hour, per worker.**

My resolution might sound like this: "Mrs. Prospect, let me ask you this way. If you could hire a better-dressed employee that visually represented your brand very well, while being safer and more comfortable while performing their job, would you be willing to pay that worker just one penny more per hour than you do today?"

Sometimes, using what is called a **TCO** or total cost of ownership breakdown, you can even get more granular on daily cost of the uniforms if the uniform lasts longer than your competitor's.

Here is how. If we look at the fact that my uniforms are not only more visually appealing but more durable and will last up to *five months longer* than my competitor's, you will see that my product is in fact less expensive than my competitor's by 78 cents each.

When you take the total cost of my product of $10,000 and divide it over the expected product life of seventeen months, and then divide that by the number of uniforms, my product costs $5.88 per uniform.

$10,000 / 17 months /100 uniforms = $5.88 each.

My competitor's price is $8,000 but the uniform's expected life is only 12 months, a full five months less than mine. When we take the $8,000 price and divide that by 12 months and then by the number of uniforms, the cost is $6.66 for each uniform, or a full 78 cents more per uniform than mine.

My TCO resolution might sound like this: Mrs. Prospect, let me ask you this way. If you could better represent your brand visually while your workers were safer and more comfortable while performing their jobs, and all it took was a slightly higher up-front investment for a solution that is overall less expensive and a better value, would you place the order today or tonight?

This tactic works more often when your product is more expensive than your competitor's, especially if your product can be broken down over end-users and expected time of product life.

<u>Tactic 6</u> – **Scarce Resources.** Any time products, services or resources are scarce, they are almost always more sought after and usually seen as more valuable, even if the scarcity is only perceived and not real. Some products are obvious scarce, such as gemstones that are difficult to find and limited in supply, but this tactic is used in marketing all of the time for everything from sandwiches to televisions, through words like "for a limited time only" or "get them while supplies last." These tactics work because they give the consumer anxiety about losing out on the goods.

As humans, we are wired to go after what we want, and if we are made to feel as if what we want will be unavailable, we typically decide or act with greater urgency. If you use this tactic, just make sure you are honest when communicating the availability of resources to the prospect; you don't want to risk your reputation by trying to create urgency with false information.

This tactic can be very effective and isn't limited to the actual product; in fact, you could leverage many different resources. Here are a few examples.

Actual inventory constraints: These include limited supplies or quantities of the total product or certain configurations of the product. You can leverage this by communicating something like this to the prospect: "Because I know you may want this product and we currently have such a limited supply, I have been authorized to hold a limited amount of inventory for your order until [insert deadline here]." Do this as long as you are able to actually manipulate the inventory and hold the product for them.

Pricing or promotions: This includes limited price reduction or special pricing for all or for certain products. In the spirit of doing what is best for the prospect, you will want to carefully communicate this as information they could use to get the best deal possible and not as a high-pressure tactic. I usually say to prospects something like this: "So you know, if you were going to move forward with a purchase, the promotional pricing ends at midnight on Friday. No pressure, I would just feel awful if you didn't get the best deal possible because no one told you about the promotion ending."

Your availability, or theirs: You may need to be available to place the order or implement the product or service with the prospect. You can leverage your availability or lack thereof, prompting the prospect to make a decision based on the scare resource of *your* availability. Conversely, the prospect might be only available during certain times, prompting them to make a decision sooner because of the scarcity of *their* availability. Learn their schedule and leverage it when possible.

Time: Use time as a scare resource whenever you can. Too many salespeople only have urgency when it's the end of their month or quarter and they need to make quota. This means nothing to the prospect as they do not typically have the same deadline to buy your product as you have to sell it.

Have urgency early so you don't have panic later.

You might be able to leverage time by discussing the time that shipping, account creation, product manufacturing, configuration or other aspects of the transaction require—or be delayed because of other factors—and use them to your advantage. You can also leverage the things in your discovery step of Understand and use the fact each day they take to decide is costing them money.

I have sent emails to prospects in stalled deals using a subject line of "$12,876.12 lost since we last met." In the body of the email, I explain how that was the total dollar amount of the lost productivity, sales, or whatever it was that I discovered during my questioning with them since we last met. The total return on investment was significantly larger, and this was just considering the three weeks or so since our last meeting when I asked for a decision.

You can also encourage them to decide by showing them that in fact, "time is money!" If you use this tactic via email to show the prospect's loss of money because of the time it is taking them to decide, like I did, it's important that this isn't the first time the prospect sees this return on invest figure, or it could have a negative impact.

Equipment: You could prompt action and a favorable decision by noting any virtual resources (such as computer servers and access to databases) or physical equipment (such as computers, vehicles, tools or other things required to sell your product) that are scarce.

Teams: In many industries, teams or even third-party involvement are required during or after the sale, so if these resources are scarce, you can use these as leverage with your prospect.

Tactic 6 works more often when the deal is stalling and the prospect is more than likely going to choose you but isn't acting with urgency.

Tactic 7 – **Comparison: The "BEN FRANKLIN."** Any time a prospect asks for a concession, ask them to consider comparing the choices considered and to prioritize the advantages of each. Use what you learned in the Understand phase of the meeting to reiterate what the prospect told you was most important and how your product or service is better for them, despite the slightly higher investment.

In this situation, you must go a little bit on the defensive and think like a defense attorney in a courtroom (the boardroom) pleading a case to a jury (the prospect). An attorney must establish reasonable doubt in order for the jury to acquit someone. While a person may not be perfect, they did not commit this particular crime. You must establish that your product, while imperfect, is still the best fit for the prospect.

Here are some things to consider:
- Does your product do things that are currently not present in the prospect's current state or that the competitor can't offer?
- Will your product solve bigger business problems?
- Will your product reduce any of the prospect's intangible concerns, such as frustration or worry?
- Will your product last longer or do something better that is important to the prospect?
- Will your product cost less in the long run because of one or more of these things listed and can you put that in another, simpler return on investment format for the prospect?

Ask the prospect to write down the benefits of the competitor's offer on the *left* side of a piece of paper. Together, you then write down all the benefits of your product on the *right*. This is again where your work in the Understand phase of the meeting will pay dividends as you should have a long (longer than the competition list) on the *right* side of the page.

Sounds simple enough, right? The tactic is called the Ben Franklin because it has been said that when Benjamin Franklin had a tough decision to make, he would narrow the options down to the top two, and then write down the benefits of each option, one on each side of a piece of paper, with a line between the two columns. He used this visual as a scale and whichever side outweighed the other was what he chose.

The Ben Franklin

The Competition

- Price
- Other small benefit
- Other small benefit

My Solution

- Huge improvement to the business
- Better Product
- Improved public image
- Improved productivity
- Other large benefit
- Other large benefit
- Other large benefit

Why always write your solution on the right side? Because it may just give you a slight psychological advantage. I did an unofficial study and found that when two products are very closely matched, the one on the right-hand side of the page is chosen more often.

I asked over 100 people of various ages to choose between two seemingly equal choices of peanut-butter brands by showing them the choices on a piece of paper, separated by a vertical line, and the option on the right was chosen over 70% of the time.

That might not seem like a big deal, but when I switched the options from left to right and asked a different set of 100 individuals, the right side was again chosen over 70% of the time, despite being a different choice than what the first hundred people chose. To me, this indicates that people, at least in my social experiment, were choosing a side more than a product.

I concluded that this has something to do with the psychology of the right choice being on the right-hand side of the page, as well as our use of the word *right* to mean both *placement* and *correct*. The fact that people overwhelmingly chose the right side over the left may just be fluke, but it seemed like a logical conclusion. In the end, fluke or not, don't take any chances—make you sure have the "right" choice on the "right side!"

Tactic 7 works more often when the prospect has narrowed down the decision between you and one of your competitors with whom you have similar or seemingly similar options, and you need to provide the prospect with a visual representation of why your product "outweighs" the competition's.

<u>Tactic 8</u> **– You can do what they can't.** Focus the customer on the facts of what your product or service can do that your competitor's can't. You should leverage that as your advantage, especially if when this attribute is a condition. If it is a hard condition that your competitor can't offer, the prospect may only be leveraging your competitor to squeeze you for a lower price.

Be careful not to become arrogant and boastful, but remain steadfast that your product is priced and positioned appropriately because of the distinct differentiation between it and its competitors.

This tactic works more often when your product has, does, or possesses something that the prospect can't get elsewhere.

<u>Tactic 9</u> – **Offer to change the configuration or terms of the offer.** Sometimes we get so wrapped up in trying to save a deal that we miss small, obvious changes. Depending on what the objection is, the answer might lie not in reconfiguring the product itself, but changing the terms of the offer. In some cases, these terms can be modified to better fit the prospect's scenario. Even if this is something you typically do in your industry, perhaps a third party could be introduced to complete the transaction. Sometimes one small change in how the deal is structured will help secure the deal. I have seen this happen when a third party was introduced to finance the initial investment and broke the deal into monthly payments in order to make a deal work.

This tactic works more often when the product—but not the terms of the offer—will work for the prospect. Think creatively and restructure the deal, if possible, to accommodate. If necessary, look at partnering with a third party to help complete the terms. Most of the time, this demonstrates your willingness to go above and beyond for the prospect, gaining you long-term loyalty and commitment.

<u>Tactic 10</u> – **Give everything you have upfront and don't back down**. You will need to have gauged what type of prospect you are dealing with quickly, if you choose this tactic, because there is no going back once it's on the table. This tactic is for the no-nonsense, time-deprived prospect who wants to get straight down to the best and final offer as quickly as possible. In this tactic, you legitimately offer everything you have upfront and explain in detail that you want the deal to progress quickly and that you do not want to invest the time needed to go back and forth to gain approvals.

That being said, you get them everything (price reduction, promotion, upgrades, etc.) you could up front so that there will be nothing more to discuss. Be sure to carefully explain that you are doing this for the benefit of time and that you realize you may be giving away more than needed to solidify the deal. Explain that you are also risking that they will ask for more and you will not have any more to give.

Again, once you use this, *you must not concede even one more thing* the prospect asks for because you will then appear to have been lying to the prospect by not offering everything upfront! If you do this correctly and carefully, explain what you have done, truly offer your concessions upfront and don't back down. As long as you have correctly judged the type of prospect, they will appreciate your honesty and your approach and move forward.

Tactic 10 is most effective when you deal with very straightforward individuals who are no-nonsense and have little time to negotiate. I use the take-it-or-leave-it approach after I have exhausted all available resources to win the deal upfront. Keep in mind that this option is typically not the most cost effective for you or your company because you will be proactively positioning every promotion, discount and other benefit you have in order to win the business.

After deploying one or more of these negotiation tactics, you will want to move back into your direct closing questions:
- "Will this option work for you?"
- "What do you think about moving forward?"
- "If I were to send over the paperwork, could we get your commitment to proceed?"
- "When would you like to start realizing these savings?"
- "If we move now, we can still meet the deadlines, so are you okay with proceeding?"

Tactic 11 – **Be sure to leverage "YOU."** If you have followed the steps so far and have done them with the utmost professionalism and value, then you should also be leveraging yourself as a negotiation tactic. After all, the competition doesn't have *you*! And if the price is higher than what the prospect wants to pay, they should add your value and worth to the equation, as well. You have value in many ways.

Here are few you can leverage:

- Experience in account management
- Unique industry knowledge
- Specific product knowledge
- Expertise in processes
- Experience solving business problems, not just product problems
- Offering a partnership as an extension of the prospect
- Offering insight and wisdom based on research and experience
- Hard work and consistently going above and beyond the standard

"I'll keep that in my notebook for safekeeping!" – Kids have school supplies and write things down.

One of my kids' favorite times of the year is just before school starts, when we go school supply shopping. They love picking out new pens and notebooks and all of the goodies that they will need for the year. In school, kids do a lot of writing, not just to develop writing skills, but also to keep track of assignments, take notes and so on.

As sales professionals, we should want to stay supremely organized, take great notes and stay on track as we run sales appointments, and especially as we adapt to new methods of selling. To do this, it is important that we adopt a sales-call plan that puts it all together for us in one place. A sales-call plan helps us stay organized, take important notes, and follow the methodology structure, which will allow us to achieve the best possible outcomes from our sales calls.

So, what does a sales-call plan look like? For some, it's a rigid set of specific tasks you must do and when you must do them, but it doesn't have to be. The one we will focus on is a very simple outline of checklists, tasks and questions I intend to ask.

Once you become accustomed to this methodology, you might just need a few prompts, such as, "Ask why they took the meeting. Ask SIIR and BART questions." The sales-call plan can either be a hard copy using paper and pen or digitally tracked and maintained on a computer or tablet. It is important that you can take notes quickly so you can focus on the prospect and keep the sales call conversational instead of something like a police interview. I will go through each part and then show you a finished copy of what mine looks like.

Let's start with the pre-meeting preparation:
- ✓ Have I *prepared* all materials I will need?
  - o Laptop
  - o Adapters for projectors/computers
  - o Power cables
  - o Notepad
  - o Pen
  - o Paperwork/Contracts
  - o Presentations print outs
  - o Leave-behinds
  - o Printed agenda for all participants
  - o Objectives and back-up objectives
  - o Verified address, time and location
  - o Research company and prospect online/social media
  - o OTHER ITEMS SPECIFIC TO YOUR BUSINESS

Next, let's take a look at the **Opening**: FIRST MEETING

- ✓ Build rapport – notice things that are *relevant* and make small talk
- ✓ Make great introductions for everyone present
- ✓ Present the agenda and objectives and explain the value I bring to them
- ✓ Ask for questions and information on any changes since I last spoke to them
- ✓ Set the stage for asking questions

I move on to the **Understand** portion of my sales meeting: <u>FIRST MEETING</u>

- ✓ Remain naturally curious and listen attentively
- ✓ WHY DID YOU DECIDE TO TAKE THIS MEETING WITH ME?
- ✓ Can you tell me about any business problems you are having? (FIND AT LEAST three)
- ✓ Ask my what, who, when, where and why questions
- ✓ Use a balance of open-ended and closed probes to get the prospect to open up about their business and business problems, wants and needs.
- ✓ Use SIIR questions to create or gather the impacts of these problems.

- ✓ **B. Buying Criteria:**
  - o What is the ideal outcome you are looking for and what will this outcome do for your business?
  - o Why was the current system chosen and has anything changed since these were the most important issues?
  - o What criteria will you use to evaluate the product you choose?
  - o What criteria will you use to evaluate the company that will provide the solution?
  - o What will you use to evaluate the ideal company representative you will choose to represent this solution?
  - o Can you list these in priority order for me, please? (LIST THE NEEDS AND WANTS IN PRIORITY ORDER)

- ✓ **A. Authority:**
  - o Can you please tell me what your decision-making process is?

- ✓ **R. Resources:**
  - o How do you typically pay for these types of services? Do you have the appropriate business paperwork such as bank credit references, articles of incorporation, etc.?

✓ **T. Timeline:**
- How soon are you looking to make a decision?
- How soon are you looking to implement the change after making your decision?

✓ What are the appropriate next steps for you?
✓ What are the appropriate next steps for me?
✓ Secure the next meeting, if appropriate

Partner portion of my sales meeting: <u>SECOND MEETING (in most cases)</u>
✓ Preparation:
- Build ROI based on answers to SIIR questions
- Build specific presentation based on prospect's problems, needs and wants in priority order
- Prepare any relevant proof that may be needed to overcome objections

✓ Present my solution with conviction by first recapping the prospect's problems, needs and wants, while reminding them what the current situation is costing them
✓ Involve the prospect in my presentation
✓ As I present, ask clarifying questions and check that the prospect understands everything I am describing and how it will benefit them
✓ Tie all of my solution's benefits back to how it will satisfy the prospect's problems
✓ Handle objections as they come
✓ Use negotiation tactics as appropriate
✓ Ask the prospect for their business (Use a date as the catalyst)
Ask CLOSING QUESTIONS

Here is a copy of what my finished sales-call planner for my first appointments looks like. I have used this or a similar version of it on every sales call for over 20 years because it works. Download this and other templates at www.mikealmorgan.com.

PHOENIX   Sales-Call Plan (First Appointment)
_____

Prospect Name_____ Date:_____
How they make money:_____

Pre-call discovery- Interesting facts learned: _____
_____   _____

Sales-call objective_____ Back-up Objective:_____

Prep Checklist: ○ Laptop   ○ Leave-behinds
                 ○ Adapters for projectors/computers   ○ Printed agenda for all participants
                 ○ Power cables   ○ Objectives and back-up objectives
                 ○ Notepad   ○ Verified address, time and location
                 ○ Pen   ○ Research company and prospect online
                 ○ Paperwork/Contracts   ○ OTHER ITEMS SPECIFIC TO YOUR BUSINESS
                 ○ Presentations print outs

❑ Small talk – Rapport
❑ Introductions
❑ Present agenda, objectives and the value I bring to them
❑ Has anything changed since we last spoke?_____
❑ Set the stage for asking questions

❑ Why did you agree to this meeting?_____

❑ Business Problem 1 –Remember to Use S.I.I.R.
_____
_____

❑ Cost or Impacts to Business _____How many times_____ #People impacted?_____

❑ Business Problem 2 –Remember to Use S.I.I.R.
_____
_____

❑ Cost or Impacts to Business _____How many times_____ #People impacted?_____

❑ Business Problem 3 –Remember to Use S.I.I.R.
_____
_____

❑ Cost or Impacts to Business _____How many times_____ #People impacted?_____

B:_____
A. _____ R. _____ T._____

❑ Recap of problems, costs, needs and wants and their impacts (both tangible and intangible)
❑ Next steps me _____ Them: _____
❑ Next Meeting date:_____

Again, your plan doesn't have to be elaborate or follow this line of questioning for everything you will ask. Often, the meeting will move in different directions and get off of an exact track. This could happen for a variety of reasons, but typically it's because the prospect asks you questions about the capability of your product or other things that may slightly derail your questioning. If the prospect's questions can be quickly answered, do so. If the answer requires a lengthy response, politely ask if you can table the question and that you will review the answer in full, along with all the specs in your presentation.

It will be up to you to use this plan to remember everything you must do and to bring the meeting back on course and get the information you need.

"You wear the cowboy hat and I will wear the cape!" – Kids role-play – You should too!

When I was kid, we played cops and robbers, cowboys and Indians, race car drivers and on and on. My kids did the same, dressing up in makeshift costumes and playing the role with conviction. Child psychology experts say that this type of play is great for children, because it exercises their imagination and gets them thinking.

Role-play does the same for us as sale-professionals. If you are like most, you hate role-play—and that *isn't* okay. In fact, you should double down on practicing these five steps so you can help more prospects, close more sales, and make more money! As is true for most anything, the more of it you do, the more comfortable with it you become.

Practicing a sales call once won't make you great, any more than going to the gym once will make you strong!

Step Four – PARTNERING WITH PROSPECTS– Recap

- Focus on solving the business problems you uncovered.
- All prospects care about FIP. Use this to build the value of your product based on how it will positively impact these topics.
- Have conviction when you tell colorful and detailed stories about how your product will impact FIP and the prospect's business problems.
- Never be afraid to use humor. People buy from people. Humor can strengthen personal connections and add value.
- Create strong, simple proposals and *present* them in person. This is when selling actually happens.
- Review your "did I?" questions and prepare accordingly to present with passion and conviction.

- Be direct with closing questions in order to finalize the sale or understand what gaps exist that you must still fill.
- Use a closing catalyst such as a date or event within the prospect organization that will instill a sense of urgency and allow the deal to progress smoothly on a defined timetable.
- Use the "should I?" questions to get the prospect to understand what questions still must be answered so that they can proceed in good faith.
- Welcome objections because they mean the sale is still alive! Use the methods prescribed for handling the specific objections identified.

I want to be your big helper!

STEP 5: SERVING AFTER THE SALE

"I want to give you something awesome!"

– Trinity (Age 5)

By the time you've reached this step, all of your hard work has begun to pay off—but you can't stop now! Service after the sale is becoming a thing of the past because of automated self-serve options, or simply poor salesmanship.

You can differentiate yourself by taking service to the next level by *serving* your clients. In this step you will learn what it takes to stand out from the rest and deliver service that builds lasting and meaningful relations that yield not only immediate sales growth by exceeding the client's expectations, but also lasting sales growth through things like introductions and referrals.

"I want to be your big helper!"– Kids don't let pride get in the way of serving others!

Kids naturally want to help and serve people. They aren't too prideful. They don't see shame in serving another person. They don't see it as beneath them.

As adults, we can learn so much from children about many things including sales, but perhaps one of the most profound things we can learn from kids is their humble willingness to shamelessly serve others. I want you to consider how rare and wonderful that trait is in a world that can be so cold, prideful and downright rude.

There are so many wonderful and beautiful things about the honest and pure nature of a child, but the absence of foolish pride is perhaps the most spectacular.

I will now share with you one of the greatest sales secrets of all times:

Serve.

This is because so few people offer what could even be considered service, and those who offer good service still aren't serving! *Serving* means more than service. Service is a basic expectation, whereas *serving* earns you loyalty and much more. So many people today are selfish, distracted and rushed that true *service* is one of the scarcest resources out there. As I explained earlier, when resources are scarce, they are typically seen as more valuable.

Clients look for that rare person who will do what they say they will do, honor every timeline, work hard on their behalf and *regularly* go the extra mile for them. Clients will reward that hard work with years of loyalty, referrals and repeat business, and will even pay a premium for products that bring top-notch service. Serving clients *the right way* is truly an advantage in future sales with the client. They will know and value what they get from you that is far and above what they get from others, so that their decision to continue to do business with you is an easy one.

Serving starts by first removing any ego and developing a *mindset* of servitude. You must also be committed to taking the time needed to serve the client in the right way. After all, you have worked so hard finding, proposing, presenting, negotiating and finalizing the deal, so why squander all of that over ego, pride or not taking the time needed to serve?

You might say, "You call them clients, but can I still call them customers?" No. *Customers* buy muffins from a bakery. *Clients* have lasting relationships with those they pay for a good or service, such as attorneys and stockbrokers. You must change the way you think about those who pay you and use terms that help you value them appropriately.

If you treat someone like a king, everyone will begin to treat them like a king.

If you refer to your customers as *clients*, you and others will begin to value them as the long-term partners they are. Again, serving starts with a mentality to serve.

"How about some ice-cold water in this cup?" - Kids are creative!

Sweat dripped down my forehead one hot day as I worked on landscaping my backyard. I was so focused on the work and on not passing out that I was startled to hear my eight-year-old son's little voice say, "Here, Dad."

The sweat stinging my eyes made it difficult to make out the large, thermal insulated mug of ice-cold water he held toward me. He handed it to me and said, "Here, Dad—I made you a bottle of water and put it in this thing, so the ice won't melt out here in the heat!"

First of all, what a kind gesture! He was so thoughtful to notice and to bring me water. What made it unique for me though, was the foresight he had to put it in an insulated cup so the ice wouldn't melt.

When we are prospecting, we should seek people who might have a "thirst" for our products—the water for me, in this example. We must stretch ourselves, however, and learn to recognize actions that allow us to go above and beyond for clients in ways that they might not even request or realize—the insulated mug.

Be creative and look for ways to add specific value to clients. Many salespeople are good about dropping by the client's office with coffee or snacks, but how many note the client's birthday and send them flowers or a personalized gift? How many care enough to learn that the client's child plays for a sports team and get them something with that team's name and colors? The bottom line is that those actions are easy and most salespeople could do them, but also that these actions don't have to cost money to serve and delight clients. In fact, many companies have policies against spending money on clients. How do you effectively serve if that's the case? You will be forced to dig deeper and think more creatively!

Ask great questions and pay attention to the details. Details matter when it comes to serving.

After explaining the *serving without spending* concept to one of the sales professionals on my team, we attended a sales call with a current client, who happened to be the Vice President of Information Technology for a very large manufacturing company. She was a brilliant lady who did a great job and appreciated our partnership.

Together, we had solved many technology-based problems and had even partnered to create cutting-edge solutions that streamlined costs and made people's lives easier at her company. In an effort to strengthen the partnership and creatively serve without spending, I asked her one of my favorite questions to ask in a sales call: "What are the biggest business problems your company faces *outside of your department?*"

She struggled, saying that she was too busy to do more than just scroll through the lists of IT projects in her mind.

I rephrased the question a bit and asked, "What do people get yelled at about around here?"

She smiled and quickly said, "Oh, staffing! Since I am not in human resources, it's not my direct problem, but because we are so severely short-staffed, there is pressure on all departments."

I asked additional questions about what they were currently doing to close the staffing gap and who else it impacted. I wanted to understand what roles they needed to fill, and why. I also probed to understand both the hard and soft costs this concern meant to the business.

She told me that they were increasing production to meet demands and had begun efforts to staff three, eight-hour shifts for a full 24-hour-a-day production schedule. She explained that since the role they needed to fill the most was that of a frontline assembly-line employee, they had some success recruiting recent graduates or students nearing graduation at the shop or technology class programs at the local high school.

She said that since these students had interest in technology and production, and had also received some basic safety skills from the school, they did quality work, adding that the retention rate was higher with those students than other sources they had tried. She went on to say that the high school recruiting program worked fine but that it was limited to the one relationship they had with their local school.

I thanked her for being so candid. She apologized, saying that it was perhaps a waste of my time since it wasn't anything for which I could offer a solution. I assured her that the time was well spent since I was interested enough to ask the questions, and that a partnership means we are in it together—her problems are my problems. I assured her we would leverage every resource to solve problems, whether we had a direct solution or not.

After the meeting, I asked my sales professional how we could serve the client based on what she told us.

"Maybe we could look at ways to deploy more technology that could help them be more efficient instead of having to hire more people," he said.

While this was good thinking for a potential long-term play, I reminded him that we uncovered that they were increasing operations to a full 24 hours a day and needed an immediate solution that required living, breathing, thinking, humans.

My sales professional looked confused and asked if we should go back in and ask additional questions.

I told him that I thought we had enough to provide some help, and then he looked really confused.
He said, "Mike, we don't sell or even know anything about staffing."

"Fair enough," I said, "but I asked you to remember the fact that we are all in the people business. It is our job to serve clients using all of our talents and resources."

We didn't know anything about staffing but are experts at using the phone and talking to people. We invested the next four hours calling on and visiting with the shop teachers in five local high schools in the surrounding area.

We coordinated with these five schools the same type of job-placement program my client had established with the one school. The next day, we called the client to let her know that in effort to best serve her, we had quadrupled her high school recruiting program. She was elated with what she called our "above and beyond" actions to solve a problem she didn't believe either of us could impact.

In full disclosure, this effort netted my team and me nothing that day. In fact, we never made a dime from going to high schools and getting them on board with a job placement program for our client.

We were, however, granted one of the largest contracts in my career about three months later on a project the same client was keeping a secret. This project did happen to be for a product we did sell.

When she called to discuss the project and how she wanted to work with us, she said, "I wanted to work with someone I could trust to always have my best interests in mind. Someone that could think creatively and take meaningful action."

To be clear, we did what we did because it was the right thing to do and we had the resources (cold-calling skills) and could serve our client. This act was done selflessly, as all acts of serving should be. It just so happens that the world has a funny way of allowing you to reap what you sow.

If you want to create lasting business relationships, then you should learn to pronounce **service** *like the client hears it—and that is*

"Serve Us!"

"I can help you better than anyone!"– Kids are competitive!

When my children were little, they competed to see who could help their mother and me better or faster. So, not only were they willing to help, but they made it into a contest of sorts. Who could mow the lawn or fold laundry the fastest? Who could get us something to drink or eat faster? Who could rake more leaves?

Just know that for sales professionals, the competition probably isn't your kid brother, but it is always there, taking the call you don't answer or responding to the email you let slip through the cracks. We must be in a race to serve clients better and faster than anyone they have ever experienced or will ever experience. You need to see it as a race, because that it exactly what it is! The only question is, who is going to win—you or them?

How can you gain a competitive advantage? While serving clients is a game of specific need fulfillment, there are some things you can do to gain an edge. Here are my ten commandments of serving.

1. **Ask your client to state the three most important things you can do as a partner to keep the relationship strong.** And then do them!

2. **Apologize sincerely if things go wrong.** Never have too much pride to say you are sorry.

3. **Be a great listener.** Actively listen, even when it isn't about your product or service.

4. **Anticipate needs and fill them proactively.** I worked for a company that charged clients for a monthly service that had the potential of using more than the contracted amount, leaving them liable for paying overage charges. As a good steward, I ran the usage reports just prior to the bill cycle for all of my clients and personally notified them that I needed to increase their plan in order to avoid any additional, surprise charges to the account. While this decreased the revenue for my company on this once instance, we recouped it by keeping a client longer since they were being served. In addition, most clients would get upset about an unexpected overage and ask for the overage to be credited anyway, so what I was getting for the higher plan charge was actually a good, long-term revenue increase and therefore good for us—and it kept the client smiling.

5. **Stay in contact.** If you are working on something for a client and you don't yet have it completed, let them know! Keep the client in the loop at all times, even if it is just to say you don't have an update. I have seen this practice gain more loyalty with clients than perhaps any other.

6. **Be an expert on your product.** Know what it can and can't do! When you know the limitations, you can properly advise a client of the deficiency and while your sale may go down, their faith in you will go up! The long-term impact will make up for that lost sale three-fold.

7. **Always have Integrity.** No matter what, be 100% honest with your clients. You will never regain trust if you lie. Most clients prefer an ugly truth to a pretty lie.

"Speak the truth, even if your voice shakes." – Maggie Kuhn

---

8. **Be tolerant and empathic.** Sometimes clients have a lot going on, like other partners to talk to, projects to work on, their own family and life problems, etc. Don't take anything personally if the client is ever short with you or doesn't return your calls or emails right away. Continue to build the relationship by being understanding and tolerant.

9. **Set the right expectations, right away.** Many times, B2B (business to business) sales professionals let this one get them in trouble. They want to be everything for the client and in some industries and some companies, that is (and should be) the case. But for most of us, we are so reluctant to tell the client that it's actually another department that will be responsible for providing things like customer service, for instance. We want to be the client's everything but most of the time that is unrealistic. Be honest upfront and tell the client what they should really expect and then help them through the process, and be available to be an escalation point.

   Most companies that hire salespeople deliberately never train them for customer service-related tasks. They want them selling, not being overpaid for performing administrative tasks. That said, customer service-related tasks may not be your job to do, but it is your job to ensure they get done.

   I always ask my sales teams, "If I were to slip and fall right in front of you, cracking my head open, would you attempt to perform surgery on me?"
   The answer was always, "No, of course not." When I would ask, "Why?" they say things like, "Because I'm not trained." Or, "I am not equipped to offer that kind of help. While my intentions would be to help you, I'm afraid I would probably kill you trying to help."

I then ask why they try to directly help a client with something they have never been trained on, or are ill-equipped to handle. When we try to help, without the right training or equipment, we run the risk of doing more harm than good. Instead, provide the right departments to the client with the proper contact information, hours or operation and expectation of assistance. And again, be there as an escalation point in case the department doesn't do what they said they would do. However, use that department and hold them accountable for their responsibility.

The same goes for expectations around things like how quickly you can return an email or call. If you are in front of clients and prospects all day, set the right expectations about when you return calls and emails. Give options like using text messaging for urgent matters. But set all of these expectations early in the relationship. In fact, I use a contact list sheet as a sales tool in the closing appointment. I let the prospect know that we have many departments filled with experts in their respective function available to serve them. The client wants help and is less particular about who in particular gives it to them, as long as they get it.

10. **Remain consistently great!** Being great is one thing. Staying great is another thing altogether. Be relentless in your pursuit to selflessly serve your clients. Consistently push yourself to "one up" your previous good deeds and levels of service.

"I love you!"– Kids only know love and must learn to hate!

You may have read this book thinking to yourself, kids can't really sell; kids get so many things they want because their mom and dad love them. Okay, but hear me out. I don't think anyone would dispute the claim that we will do more for those we love, so the real question is, how do you get the prospect or client to love you?

First ask yourself if you love the client. If not, learn to. After all, they are paying for you to live. It was more than *your* ability to sell them something, it also was *their* decision to buy that pays your mortgage, car payment, food and so on. We need to all appreciate that and treat the client accordingly.

Hone your skills and practice your craft, but if you really want to win long-term in sales, learn to love. **Love** the client. **Love** to get out there in front of prospects (even if you are rejected—*a lot*) and learn to **love** the process and the grind. **Love** artfully by asking questions and creating the perfect proposal. Learn to **love** the butterflies you feel when you present your solution. And **love** the fact that some sales take more time than others.

"Kids will go where there is excitement and stay where there is love."

– Zig Ziglar

So will clients!

Step Five – SERVING AFTER THE SALE– Recap

- Don't let pride get in the way of serving others!
- Have a mindset of serving clients and prospects.
- Don't wait until they become a client to start serving.
- There is a difference between service and serving. Serving differentiates you while adding value to the client.
- Be creative and proactive in your approach.
- See service as a competitive sport because it is and your goal should be to win.
- Follow my ten commandments for serving clients.
- Learn to **love** the process, the grind, the clients and your profession.

RESOURCES

(1) Page 4 - 1/10/2019
Source: https://hbr.org/2015/01/companies-with-a-formal-sales-process-generate-more-revenue

(2) Page 4 – 1/12-2019
Source: http://www.dealmakerindex.com/Hermes/

(3) Page 69 – 11/02/2019
Source: https://en.wikipedia.org/wiki/Socratic_questioning

MORE THAN AN EVENT, REAL BUSINESS RESULTS!

Are you looking to add value and excitement to your next sales meeting? Let me come out and deliver a high-energy, value-packed, keynote presentation! OR get your teams fully trained to exceed sales goals by booking a full 5-Step Sales Training©, today!

Easy to understand | Easy to coach to | Immediate ROI

Depending on what you need covered, I will teach your team some or all of how to:

- **Speed up the sales process** by setting meaningful appointments with the most qualified prospects.
- **Close more sales** by properly opening a sales call with purpose, structure and meaning.
- **Close bigger sales, faster** by asking better questions, listening to, and understanding prospects like never before by digging deep the *right* way.
- *Maintain* **high sale results** by properly managing a sales funnel.
- **Unstick, stuck sales** by partnering with colorful storytelling, dynamic, ROI-based presentations, shrewd negotiations and win-win closes.
- **Build lasting business relationships** that yield incremental business and referrals.

To schedule a program before it fills up for the date you need, please visit www.mikealmorgan.com today or call me directly at: +1 281-615-7810

And finally, I would like to sincerely thank you for buying this book. I hope you learned and smiled along the way, and that the information I shared brings you closer to your sales goals.

All my best,
Mikeal R. Morgan

Made in the USA
Coppell, TX
27 September 2020

38938430R00085